초등학생의 영어 친구

# 그래머버디
## GRAMMAR BUDDY

**2**

# 그래머버디 2

| | |
|---|---|
| **지은이** | NE능률 영어교육연구소 |
| **연구원** | 한정은, 이설미, 장민아, 박효빈 |
| **영문 교열** | Lewis Hugh Hosie, Peter Morton, MyAn Le |
| **디자인** | 장현정, 김연주 |
| **내지 일러스트** | 이지원, 강주연, 마이신, 유경민, 류미선, 바나나비 |
| **내지 사진** | www.shutterstock.com |
| **맥편집** | 이정화 |
| **영업** | 한기영, 이경구, 박인규, 정철교, 하진수, 김남준, 이우현 |
| **마케팅** | 박혜선, 남경진, 이지원, 김여진 |

42
nd
Since 1980
Let's grow together

# NE능률이
# 미래를
# 창조합니다.

건강한 배움의 고객가치를 제공하겠다는 꿈을 실현하기 위해
42년 동안 열심히 달려왔습니다.

앞으로도 끊임없는 연구와 노력을 통해
당연한 것을 멈추지 않고

고객, 기업, 직원 모두가 함께 성장하는 NE능률이 되겠습니다.

**Dear Friends,**

I'm your English Buddy!
Forget about all your worries.
I'm here to help you!
Let's smile! Let's learn! And let's have fun!

All the best,
Your English Buddy

# ★ HOW TO USE ★

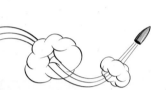

### 다시 보기
새로운 Unit을 시작하기 전에, 지난 Unit에서 배운 내용을 한 번 더 확인해 보세요.

### 미리 보기
새로운 Unit에서 배울 내용을 만화를 통해 미리 살펴보세요.

### 문법 활용 스토리
쉽고 재미있는 스토리를 읽고, 그 속에 녹아 있는 문법을 찾아보세요.

### 핵심 문법 POINT
처음 문법을 시작하는 학생들이 꼭 알아야 할 문법을 알기 쉽게 설명하였습니다. 풍부한 예문을 통해 문법 이해와 흥미를 높이세요.

### CHECK UP
학습한 문법은 간단한 문제로 바로 확인해 보세요.

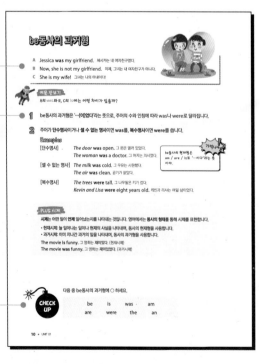

### 기억나
학습 내용과 관련된 문법 포인트를 다시 짚어주어 반복 학습이 가능합니다.

### BUDDY'S TIPS
초등학생들이 헷갈리기 쉬운 문법포인트를 콕 집어 설명하였습니다.

### PLUS
학습한 문법에서 한 걸음 더 나아가 보세요.

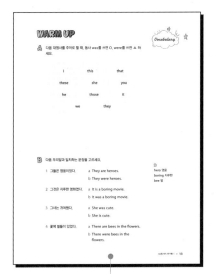

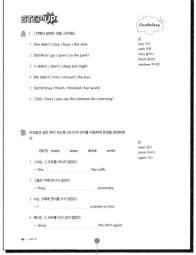

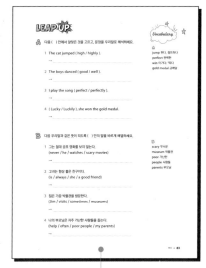

## WARM UP

간단한 유형의 기본 문제를 통해 학습한 문법을 확인해 보세요!

## STEP UP

Warm up 보다 한 단계 높은 문제를 풀면서, 문법을 활용하는 힘을 길러 보세요.

## LEAP UP

다양한 형태의 쓰기 문제를 통해 문장 쓰기의 기초를 다져 보세요. 중학교 내신 서술형 문제에도 함께 대비할 수 있어요.

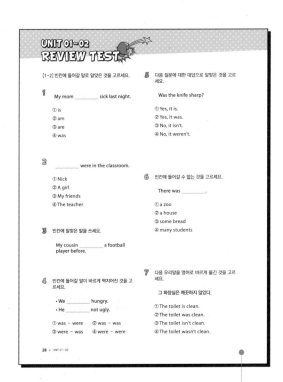

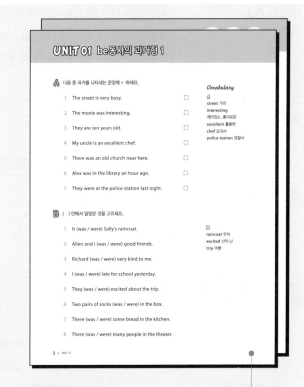

## REVIEW TEST

두 개 Unit을 공부한 후, 객관식 유형과 주관식 유형을 통해 학습한 내용을 종합적으로 확인해 보세요.

## WORKBOOK

본문에서 부족한 문제는 워크북을 통해 보충해 보세요. Drill, 쓰기 연습 등 다양한 유형으로 문법을 연습할 수 있습니다.

# ☆ CONTENTS ☆

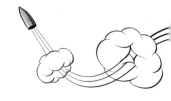

**Level 3**

# ★ 기초 다지기 ★

품사
수많은 영어 단어들을 공통된 성질에 따라 묶어 종류별로 나눈 것을 '품사'라고 합니다.

## 1 명사

세상의 모든 것은 이름을 가지고 있습니다. '학교', '책', '사랑', '공기'처럼 사람이나 사물의 이름을 나타내는 말을 명사라고 합니다.

**Examples**     Amy 에이미   school 학교   song 노래   pencil 연필   park 공원

## 2 대명사

명사를 대신하는 말을 대명사라고 합니다. 이름을 말하지 않고도 '너', '우리', '이것', '저것'과 같은 대명사를 통해 의미를 전달할 수 있습니다.

**Examples**     I 나   you 너   he 그   this 이것   that 저것

## 3 동사

동사는 사람이나 사물의 동작이나 상태를 나타내는 말입니다. 우리말로는 '먹다', '가다', '있다'와 같은 말들이 바로 동사입니다.

**Examples**     eat 먹다   go 가다   have 가지다   sing 노래하다

## 4 형용사

형용사는 명사의 생김새나 기분, 상태 등을 구체적으로 설명해 주는 말입니다. 우리말로는 '큰', '행복한', '아픈' 같은 말들이 바로 형용사입니다.

**Examples**     big 큰   small 작은   happy 행복한   sunny 화창한

## 5 부사

부사는 언제, 어디서, 어떻게, 얼마나 등을 나타내어 문장의 의미를 풍부하게 해 주는 말입니다. 우리말로는 '빠르게', '매우' 같은 말들이 바로 부사입니다.

**Examples**     slowly 느리게   fast 빠르게   easily 쉽게   very 매우

## 6  전치사

전치사는 명사나 대명사 앞에 쓰여서 장소나 위치, 시간 등을 나타내는 말입니다. 우리말로는 '…뒤에', '… 후에'와 같은 말들이 바로 전치사입니다.

**Examples**    in … 안에    on … 위에    behind … 뒤에    next to … 옆에

## 7  접속사

접속사는 단어와 단어 또는 문장과 문장을 연결해 주는 말로, 말과 말 사이를 매끄럽게 이어주는 역할을 합니다. 우리말의 '그리고', '그러나', '그래서' 같은 말들이 바로 접속사입니다.

**Examples**    and 그리고    but 그러나    so 그래서    after … 후에

# SPEED CHECK

**A**  명사에는 O, 대명사에는 △ 하세요.

rabbit    we    rose    bed

this    it    Seoul    I

**B**  다음 단어와 품사를 바르게 연결하세요.

1 over  •              • a  형용사

2 small  •             • b  전치사

3 we  •                • c  대명사

**C**  빈칸에 알맞은 말을 쓰세요.

1 _____ 은(는) 사람이나 사물의 이름을 나타내는 말입니다.

2 _____ 은(는) 사람이나 사물의 동작이나 상태를 나타냅니다.

3 _____ 은(는) 단어와 단어 또는 문장과 문장을 연결해 주는 말입니다.

# UNIT 01 — be동사의 과거형 1

## 미리 보기

만화를 통해 이번 Unit에서 배울 내용을 미리 살펴보세요.

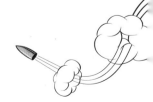

# be동사의 과거형

**A** Jessica **was** my girlfriend.   제시카는 내 여자친구였다.

**B** Now, she is not my girlfriend.   이제, 그녀는 내 여자친구가 아니다.

**C** She is my wife! 그녀는 나의 아내이다!

## 예문 맛보기

A의 was와 B, C의 is에는 어떤 차이가 있을까?

**1** be동사의 과거형은 '···(이)었다'라는 뜻으로, 주어의 수와 인칭에 따라 was나 were로 달라집니다.

**2** 주어가 **단수명사**이거나 **셀 수 없는 명사**이면 **was**를, **복수명사**이면 **were**를 씁니다.

### Examples

[단수명사]   *The door* **was** open. 그 문은 열려 있었다.

　　　　　　*The woman* **was** a doctor. 그 여자는 의사였다.

[셀 수 없는 명사]   *The milk* **was** cold. 그 우유는 시원했다.

　　　　　　*The air* **was** clean. 공기가 맑았다.

[복수명사]   *The trees* **were** tall. 그 나무들은 키가 컸다.

　　　　　　*Kevin and Lisa* **were** eight years old. 케빈과 리사는 여덟 살이었다.

> 기억나!?
> be동사의 현재형은
> am / are / is로 '···이다'라는 뜻
> 이야.

## PLUS 시제

**시제**는 어떤 일이 **언제** 일어났는지를 나타내는 것입니다. 영어에서는 **동사의 형태**를 통해 시제를 표현합니다.

• 현재시제: 늘 일어나는 일이나 현재의 사실을 나타내며, 동사의 현재형을 사용합니다.

• 과거시제: 이미 지나간 과거의 일을 나타내며, 동사의 과거형을 사용합니다.

The movie **is** funny. 그 영화는 **재미있다**. (현재시제)

The movie **was** funny. 그 영화는 **재미있었다**. (과거시제)

다음 중 be동사의 과거형에 ○ 하세요.

**CHECK UP**

be　　　is　　　was　　　am

are　　　were　　　the　　　an

# WARM UP

**Vocabulary**

 **A** 다음 중 과거를 나타내는 문장에 ✓ 하세요.

1  EXO is popular.  ☐

2  Olivia is a clever girl.  ☐

3  The streets were clean.  ☐

4  My parents are healthy.  ☐

5  The cat is in the box.  ☐

6  Steve was a baseball player.  ☐

7  The neighbors were friendly.  ☐

8  The movie was interesting.  ☐

Ⓐ
popular 인기 있는
clever 똑똑한
street 거리
healthy 건강한
baseball player
야구선수
neighbor 이웃
friendly 친절한
interesting 재미있는

**B** ( ) 안에서 알맞은 것을 고르세요.

1  The castle ( was / were ) big.

2  Her hands ( was / were ) warm.

3  The sea ( was / were ) beautiful.

4  The computer ( was / were ) old.

5  The questions ( was / were ) easy.

6  The apples ( was / were ) fresh.

Ⓑ
castle 성, 성곽
hand 손
question 질문, 문제
easy 쉬운
fresh 신선한

# 대명사 주어와 be동사의 과거형

A  Last night, I **was** alone at home.  어젯밤, 나는 집에 혼자 있었다.

B  Two thieves came into my house.  도둑 두 명이 집에 들어왔다.

C  They **were** very scary!  그들은 매우 무서웠다!

**예문 맛보기**

A의 I 뒤에는 was가, C의 They 뒤에는 were가 쓰인 이유는 뭘까?

**1** 주어가 대명사일 때, be동사의 과거형은 주어에 따라 달라집니다. 이때 주어와 be동사의 과거형은 줄여 쓰지 않습니다.

|  | 주어 | be동사의 과거형 |
|---|---|---|
| 단수 | I | was |
|  | You | were |
|  | He / She / It | was |
| 복수 | You / We / They | were |

**BUDDY'S TIPS**
주어가 this, that일 때는 was를, these, those일 때는 were를 써.

**Examples**

I **was** thirsty. 나는 목이 말랐다.

He **was** a baker. 그는 제빵사였다.

You **were** pretty. 너는 예뻤다.

We **were** hungry. 우리는 배고팠다.

**2** 「**There was/were + 주어**」는 '…이 있었다'라는 의미입니다. 주어로 단수명사나 셀 수 없는 명사가 오면 was를, 복수명사가 오면 were를 사용합니다.

**Examples**

There **was** *a man*. 한 남자가 있었다.

There **were** *frogs*. 개구리들이 있었다.

**PLUS 과거를 나타내는 표현**

다음 표현들을 이용하면 과거에 일어난 일을 더 정확하게 표현할 수 있습니다.

yesterday 어제          last night/week/month/year 지난밤/주/달/해

… ago … 전에          before 전에

I was busy **yesterday**. 나는 어제 바빴다.

She was poor **two years ago**. 그녀는 2년 전에 가난했다.

# WARM UP

*Vocabulary*

 다음 대명사를 주어로 할 때, 동사 was를 쓰면 O, were를 쓰면 △ 하세요.

I      this      that

these      she      you

he      those      it

we      they

 다음 우리말과 일치하는 문장을 고르세요.

1 그들은 영웅이었다.
    a They are heroes.
    b They were heroes.

2 그것은 지루한 영화였다.
    a It is a boring movie.
    b It was a boring movie.

3 그녀는 귀여웠다.
    a She was cute.
    b She is cute.

4 꽃에 벌들이 있었다.
    a There was bees in the flowers.
    b There were bees in the flowers.

B
hero 영웅
boring 지루한
bee 벌

 **A** ( ) 안에서 알맞은 것을 고르세요.

*Vocabulary*

Ⓐ
sad 슬픈
now 지금
festival 축제
dream 꿈
last 지난
poor 가난한
before 전에
delicious 맛있는
gym 체육관
playground
운동장, 놀이터

1 He ( is / was ) sad now.

2 The festival ( was / were ) fun.

3 It ( was / were ) a happy dream.

4 Last winter ( is / was ) very cold.

5 They ( are / were ) poor before.

6 The apple pies ( was / were ) delicious.

7 Julia ( was / were ) at the gym yesterday.

8 The children ( was / were ) in the playground.

**B** 빈칸에 알맞은 말을 〈보기〉에서 골라 쓰세요.

Ⓑ
tired 피곤한
nervous 불안해하는
every day 매일
these days 요즘에는

| 〈보기〉 | am | is | are | was | were |
|---|---|---|---|---|---|

1 She _____ tired last night.

2 I _____ very nervous now.

3 The store _____ open every day.

4 The Webtoons _____ popular these days.

5 They _____ famous singers two years ago.

C 다음 우리말과 같은 뜻이 되도록 빈칸에 알맞은 말을 쓰세요.

C
firefighter 소방관
brave 용감한
classmate 반 친구
bottle 병

1 그 소방관들은 용감했다.

→ The firefighters _____ brave.

2 우리는 반 친구였다.

→ We _____ classmates.

3 그는 똑똑하고 친절했다.

→ He _____ smart and friendly.

4 병 안에 약간의 물이 있었다.

→ There _____ some water in the bottle.

D 다음 빈칸에 was나 were 중 알맞은 것을 쓰세요.

D
zoo 동물원
with …와 함께
lion 사자
excited 신이 난

1 I _____ at the zoo.
2 Paul _____ with me.
3 There _____ lions.
4 They _____ very big!
5 We _____ very excited.

**E** 다음 그림을 보고 〈보기〉의 단어와 be동사를 이용하여 문장을 완성하세요.

**2006**　　　　　**Now**

〈보기〉　short　　blue　　tall　　yellow

1 I _____ _____ in 2006.

2 Now, I _____ _____.

3 The roller coaster _____ _____ then.

4 Now, it _____ _____.

**F** 다음 문장에서 밑줄 친 부분을 바르게 고쳐 쓰세요.

1 The place <u>is</u> clean yesterday.　　→ _____

2 Charlie <u>were</u> a reporter in the past.　　→ _____

3 The bus <u>were</u> full ten minutes ago.　　→ _____

4 The windows <u>are</u> open an hour ago.　　→ _____

5 Sue and David <u>was</u> my neighbors last year.

→ _____

**A** 다음 문장을 과거시제 문장으로 다시 쓰세요.

1 You are a good designer.

→ _____

2 Romeo is in love with Juliet.

→ _____

3 This is a birthday present from Andy.

→ _____

4 There are some restaurants on this street.

→ _____

**B** 주어진 말을 이용하여 우리말에 맞게 영작하세요.

1 나는 매우 바빴다. (I, very busy)

→ _____

2 그녀는 사랑스러운 소녀였다. (she, a lovely girl)

→ _____

3 그것은 그의 자전거였다. (it, his bicycle)

→ _____

4 그들은 공항에 있었다. (they, at the airport)

→ _____

5 우리는 배고프고 추웠다. (we, hungry and cold)

→ _____

# 지각하는 이유

매일 지각을 하는 학생이 있었다.
화가 난 선생님은 며칠을
벼르다가 야단을 쳤다.

넌 어쩌면
개학 첫날부터 지금까지
매일 지각이니?

선생님께서
규칙적인 생활을 하라고
하셨잖아요..!!

# be동사의 과거형 2: 부정문과 의문문

지난 Unit에서 배운 내용을 다시 확인해 보세요.

☆ **be동사의 과거형**

I **was** thirsty. 나는 목이 말랐다.

You **were** pretty. 너는 예뻤다.

He **was** a baker. 그는 제빵사였다.

The woman **was** a doctor. 그 여자는 의사였다.

The trees **were** tall. 그 나무들은 키가 컸다.

There **was** a man. 한 남자가 있었다.

There **were** frogs. 개구리들이 있었다.

만화를 통해 이번 Unit에서 배울 내용을 미리 살펴보세요.

# 부정문 만들기: be동사의 과거형

A  I had a party yesterday.  나는 어제 파티를 열었다.

B  The party **was not** fun.  그 파티는 재미가 없었다.

C  Jenny **wasn't** at my party.  제니가 내 파티에 없었다.

D  She was at Eric's party.  그녀는 에릭의 파티에 있었다.

**예문맛보기**

B와 C는 was를 사용한 부정문이야. 이 두 문장이 D와 어떻게 다른지 비교해 봐.

**1** be동사 과거형의 부정문은 was, were 뒤에 not을 붙인 「**주어+was/were+not ….**」의 형태로, '**…이 아니었다**'라고 해석합니다.

She **was** at home. → She **was** at home.  You **were** short. → You **were** short.
그녀는 집에 있었다.　　　그녀는 집에 없었다.　　　너는 키가 작았다.　　　너는 키가 작지 않았다.

**Examples**

I **was not** sad. 나는 슬프지 않았다.

They **were not** rich. 그들은 부유하지 않았다.

The prince **was not** smart. 그 왕자는 똑똑하지 않았다.

The stories **were not** interesting. 그 이야기들은 재미없었다.

**2** was not과 were not은 다음과 같이 줄여 쓸 수 있습니다.

was not → **wasn't**　　were not → **weren't**

**BUDDY'S TIPS**
be동사의 부정형은 항상 be동사 뒤에 not을 붙여.
· 현재형: 「am/are/is + not」
· 과거형: 「was/were + not」

**Examples**

She **wasn't** good at math. 그녀는 수학을 잘하지 못했다.

They **weren't** classmates. 그들은 반 친구가 아니었다.

The tea **wasn't** hot. 그 차는 따뜻하지 않았다.

The wallets **weren't** cheap. 그 지갑들은 값이 싸지 않았다.

**CHECK UP**

다음 밑줄 친 부분의 줄임형으로 알맞은 것을 고르세요.

1  Charlie <u>was not</u> tired.　　① isn't　　② wasn't

2  We <u>were not</u> hungry.　　① aren't　　② weren't

3  The man <u>was not</u> weak.　　① wasn't　　② weren't

# WARM UP

**A** 다음 중 be동사 과거형의 부정문에 ✓ 하세요.

1 He was on holiday. ☐

2 Turtles are not fast. ☐

3 You were not short. ☐

4 The tea was not hot. ☐

5 The beds were not soft. ☐

6 The prince was not weak. ☐

7 The comedy movie was funny. ☐

8 The men were not in the office. ☐

A
on holiday
휴가 중인
turtle 거북
hot 뜨거운
soft 부드러운, 푹신한
weak 약한
comedy movie
코미디 영화
office 사무실

**B** 다음 문장에서 not이 들어갈 위치에 ✓ 하세요.

1 Daniel ① was ② sick ③.

2 We ① were ② surprised ③.

3 They ① were ② on ③ the bus.

4 The ① cheese ② was ③ fresh.

5 My mother ① was ② a nurse ③.

6 The ① waiters ② were ③ friendly.

7 The moon ① was ② bright ③ last night.

# 의문문 만들기: be동사의 과거형

**A**  **Were you** at the concert?  너 그 공연장에 있었니?

**B**  **Yes**, I **was**.  응, 있었어.

**C**  **Was the singer** good?  그 가수는 잘했니?

**D**  **No**, he **wasn't**.  아니, 잘하지 못했어.

### 예문 맛보기

be동사의 과거형을 사용해서 질문할 때는 A, C처럼 Were나 Was로 시작해!

**1**  be동사 과거형의 의문문은 be동사와 주어의 위치를 바꾼 「**Was/Were+주어 …?**」의 형태로, '**…이었니?**'라고 해석합니다.

**Jerry  was**  fast. 제리가 빨랐다.

**Was  Jerry**  fast? 제리가 빨랐니?

**They  were**  free  yesterday. 그들은 어제 한가했다.

**Were  they**  free  yesterday? 그들은 어제 한가했니?

### Examples

**Was he** a bus driver? 그는 버스 운전기사였니?

**Were you** with your friends? 너는 친구들과 있었니?

**Was Britney** famous before? 브리트니가 전에는 유명했니?

**Were the models** in New York? 그 모델들은 뉴욕에 있었니?

**2**  be동사 과거형의 의문문에는 다음과 같이 대답합니다.

| 긍정 대답 | 부정 대답 |
|---|---|
| **Yes**, 주어+**was/were**. | **No**, 주어+**wasn't/weren't**. |

### Examples

A: Was he late yesterday? 어제 그가 늦었니?

B: **Yes**, he **was**. 응, 늦었어. / **No**, he **wasn't**. 아니, 안 늦었어.

A: Were the boxes heavy? 그 상자들은 무거웠니?

B: **Yes**, they **were**. 응, 무거웠어. / **No**, they **weren't**. 아니, 안 무거웠어.

# WARM UP

**A** 다음 중 be동사 과거형의 의문문에 ✓ 하세요.

1  Is she a ballerina? ☐

2  Were they at school? ☐

3  Are the boxes heavy? ☐

4  Were you sad yesterday? ☐

5  Is the woman your teacher? ☐

6  Was he happy with the gift? ☐

**B** 다음 빈칸에 들어갈 말로 알맞은 것을 고르세요.

1  _____ his house clean?　　① Was　② Were

2  _____ you absent today?　　① Was　② Were

3  _____ the streets crowded?　① Was　② Were

4  A: Was the soup delicious?
   B: Yes, it _____.　　① was　② were

5  A: Were they here last night?
   B: No, they _____.　　① wasn't　② weren't

6  A: Were you with your family?
   B: Yes, I _____.　　① was　② were

 ( ) 안에서 알맞은 것을 고르세요.

1 They ( were'nt / weren't ) ready.

2 ( Was / Is ) he outside last night?

3 I ( was not / not was ) angry at him.

4 The game ( wasn't / weren't ) exciting.

5 ( Was / Were ) you in the restroom?

6 We ( aren't / weren't ) late for the last class.

**A**
ready 준비가 된
outside 밖에
angry 화난
exciting
신나는, 흥미진진한
restroom 화장실

**B** ( ) 안에서 알맞은 것을 고르고, 빈칸에 알맞은 줄임형을 쓰세요.

1 He ( was / were ) not a scientist.

→ He ___wasn't___ a scientist.

2 My uncle ( was / were ) not upset.

→ My uncle _____ upset.

3 The cherries ( was / were ) not fresh.

→ The cherries _____ fresh.

4 They ( was / were ) not my favorite soccer team.

→ They _____ my favorite soccer team.

5 Tom and Joli ( was / were ) not at the coffee shop.

→ Tom and Joli _____ at the coffee shop.

**B**
scientist 과학자
upset 속상한
cherry 체리
favorite
매우 좋아하는
coffee shop 커피숍

**C** 다음 그림을 보고 빈칸에 알맞은 말을 쓰세요.

1

I ___wasn't___ scared.

I ___was___ brave.

2

They _____ in Tokyo.

They _____ in Paris.

3

He _____ hungry.

He _____ full.

4

We _____ sleepy.

We _____ excited.

**C**
scared
겁먹은, 무서워하는
Tokyo 도쿄
full 배부르게 먹은
sleepy 졸린

**D** 우리말과 같은 뜻이 되도록 주어진 단어를 이용하여 문장을 완성하세요.

1 그 자동차는 빨랐니? (fast)

→ _____ the car _____ ?

2 네 부모님이 행복해 하셨니? (happy)

→ _____ your parents _____ ?

3 그 예술가는 부유하지 않았다. (rich)

→ The artist _____ _____ _____ .

4 그 의자들은 편안하지 않았다. (comfortable)

→ The chairs _____ _____ _____ .

**D**
fast 빠른
happy 행복한
artist 화가, 예술가
comfortable
편안한

**E** 다음 그림을 보고 빈칸에 알맞은 말을 쓰세요.

**Vocabulary**

**E**
mall 시장, 쇼핑몰

**Last Sunday**

| Tony | Andy | Jack and Ann |

1 A: _____Was Tony_____ sick last Sunday?

   B: Yes, _____ .

2 A: _____ at the gym last Sunday?

   B: _____

3 A: _____ at the mall last Sunday?

   B: _____

**F** 다음 문장에서 <u>틀린</u> 부분을 찾아 바르게 고쳐 쓰세요.

**F**
loud 시끄러운
quiz 퀴즈, 시험
difficult 어려운

1 Was sleepy the dog?

2 His feet wasn't clean.

3 The music wasnt loud.

4 The quiz not was difficult.

5 My teacher were not angry.

6 The ice cream weren't sweet.

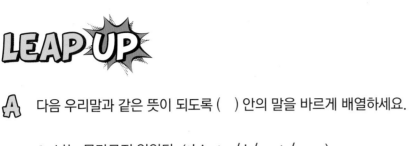

A 다음 우리말과 같은 뜻이 되도록 ( ) 안의 말을 바르게 배열하세요.

1 나는 목마르지 않았다. (thirsty / I / not / was)

→ _____

2 그 표들은 비쌌니? (expensive / the tickets / were)

→ _____

3 그 신발은 새 것이 아니었다. (were / the shoes / new / not)

→ _____

4 너희 어머니는 변호사이셨니? (your mother / was / a lawyer)

→ _____

B 다음 문장을 ( ) 안의 지시대로 바꿔 쓰세요.

1 The meal was tasty. (부정문)

→ _____

2 Jimmy was hurt. (의문문)

→ _____

3 The children were noisy. (부정문)

→ _____

4 His grandfather was a teacher. (의문문)

→ _____

# UNIT 01~02
## REVIEW TEST

[1–2] 빈칸에 들어갈 말로 알맞은 것을 고르세요.

**1**

My mom _____ sick last night.

① is
② am
③ are
④ was

**2**

_____ were in the classroom.

① Nick
② A girl
③ My friends
④ The teacher

**3** 빈칸에 알맞은 말을 쓰세요.

My cousin _____ a football player before. He was a baseball player.

**4** 빈칸에 들어갈 말이 바르게 짝지어진 것을 고르세요.

• We _____ hungry.
• He _____ not ugly.

① was – were    ② was – was
③ were – was    ④ were – were

**5** 다음 질문에 대한 대답으로 알맞은 것을 고르세요.

Was the knife sharp?

① Yes, it is.
② Yes, it was.
③ No, it isn't.
④ No, it weren't.

**6** 빈칸에 들어갈 수 <u>없는</u> 것을 고르세요.

There was _____.

① a zoo
② a house
③ some bread
④ many students

**7** 다음 우리말을 영어로 바르게 옮긴 것을 고르세요.

그 화장실은 깨끗하지 않았다.

① The toilet is clean.
② The toilet was clean.
③ The toilet isn't clean.
④ The toilet wasn't clean.

All our dreams can come true,
if we have the courage to pursue them.

– Walt Disney

**8** 빈칸에 들어갈 말이 다른 하나를 고르세요.

① I _____ on the bus an hour ago.

② The cats _____ small last year.

③ The wind _____ not strong yesterday.

④ The house _____ not empty last month.

**12** 다음 문장을 의문문으로 바꿀 때 빈칸에 알맞은 말을 쓰세요.

The pictures were wonderful.

→ _____ wonderful?

[9-10] 다음 중 틀린 문장을 고르세요.

**9** ① The sky was dark.

② The lion was scary.

③ They weren't young.

④ We not were at the park.

[13-14] 다음 우리말과 같은 뜻이 되도록 빈칸에 알맞은 말을 쓰세요.

**13** 그 토마토는 싱싱하지 않았다.

→ The tomato _____ _____ fresh.

**10** ① Are you tired now?

② Is Harry alone yesterday?

③ Was your brother angry with me?

④ Was the restaurant open last Sunday?

**14** 소파 위에 잡지들이 있었다.

→ _____ _____ magazines on the sofa.

**11** 빈칸에 알맞은 말을 쓰세요.

A: Was Kate your roommate?

B: No, she _____.

**15** 다음 문장에서 틀린 부분을 찾아 바르게 고쳐 쓰세요.

Were the weather nice yesterday?

→ _____ → _____

# 나는야 탐험가

신비한 고대 문명의 비밀을 파헤치기 위해 떠나볼까요?
탐험을 위해 필요한 도구들을 찾아주세요.
돋보기, 망원경, 수첩, 펜, 카메라, 모자

(정답은 p.127에서 확인할 수 있습니다.)

# 일반동사의 과거형 1

 **다시 보기**

지난 Unit에서 배운 내용을 다시 확인해 보세요.

☆ **be동사 과거형의 부정문**

The prince **was not** smart. 그 왕자는 똑똑하지 않았다.

The stories **were not** interesting. 그 이야기들은 재미없었다.

She **wasn't** good at math. 그녀는 수학을 잘하지 못했다.

They **weren't** classmates. 그들은 반 친구가 아니었다.

☆ **be동사 과거형의 의문문**

A: **Was he** late yesterday? 어제 그가 늦었니?

B: **Yes**, he **was**. 응, 늦었어. / **No**, he **wasn't**. 아니, 안 늦었어.

A: **Were the boxes** heavy? 그 상자들은 무거웠니?

B: **Yes**, they **were**. 응, 무거웠어. / **No**, they **weren't**. 아니, 안 무거웠어.

 **미리 보기**

만화를 통해 이번 Unit에서 배울 내용을 미리 살펴보세요.

# 일반동사의 과거형

**A** Jack **lived** next door to me.  잭은 나의 옆집에 살았다.

**B** We always **played** together.  우리는 항상 함께 놀았다.

**C** Now he lives in another city.  이제 그는 다른 도시에 산다.

**D** I miss him very much.  나는 그가 정말 많이 그립다.

### 예문 맛보기

A의 lived와 B의 played는 각각 동사 live와 play의 과거형이야.

**1** 일반동사를 사용하여 과거의 일을 나타낼 때는 **일반동사의 과거형**을 쓰고, '…했다'라고 해석합니다. 일반동사의 과거형을 만들 때는 주로 규칙을 따르지만, 불규칙적으로 변하는 동사들도 있습니다.

**2** **규칙 변화**: 일반동사는 대체로 다음과 같은 규칙에 따라 과거형으로 변합니다.

| 동사의 형태 | 규칙 | Examples | |
|---|---|---|---|
| 대부분의 동사 | 동사원형+-ed | call – call**ed**<br>play – play**ed** | visit – visit**ed**<br>watch – watch**ed** |
| -e로 끝나는 동사 | 동사원형+-d | love – love**d**<br>dance – dance**d** | arrive – arrive**d**<br>close – close**d** |
| 「자음+y」로 끝나는 동사 | y를 i로 고치고<br>+-ed | try – tr**ied**<br>study – stud**ied** | cry – cr**ied**<br>dry – dr**ied** |
| 「단모음+단자음」으로<br>끝나는 동사 | 맨 뒤 자음을 한 번<br>더 쓰고 +-ed | plan – plan**ned**<br>stop – stop**ped** | drop – drop**ped**<br>shop – shop**ped** |

### Examples

My teacher **called** my name. 선생님이 내 이름을 불렀다.
William **closed** the window. 윌리엄은 창문을 닫았다.
I **studied** very hard. 나는 매우 열심히 공부했다.
They **shopped** at the market. 그들은 시장에서 쇼핑을 했다.

> **BUDDY'S TIPS**
> 일반동사의 과거형은 주어의 인칭과 수에 따라 모양이 달라지지 않아.

### PLUS 항상 과거시제를 사용하는 경우

역사 속에서 일어난 일을 나타낼 때는 항상 과거시제를 사용합니다.

Mozart **played** the piano well. 모차르트는 피아노를 잘 쳤다.
Bell **invented** the telephone in 1876. 벨은 1876년에 전화기를 발명했다.

# WARM UP

**A** 다음 문장에서 일반동사의 과거형에 밑줄을 그으세요.

1  We waited for you.

2  Our cat hated baths.

3  I dropped my pencil.

4  He closed the door.

5  Peter visited a museum.

6  The boy studied English.

7  She loved her boyfriend.

A
wait 기다리다
hate 싫어하다
bath 목욕
drop 떨어뜨리다
close 닫다
museum 박물관
study 공부하다

**B** 다음 일반동사의 과거형으로 알맞은 것을 고르세요.

1  try      ① tried      ② tryed

2  dry      ① dryed      ② dried

3  talk     ① talkied     ② talked

4  stay     ① stayed      ② staied

5  dance    ① danced      ② dancd

6  plan     ① planed      ② planned

7  watch    ① watched     ② watchied

8  arrive   ① arriveed    ② arrived

B
try 노력하다
dry 말리다
talk 말하다,
이야기하다
stay 머물다
plan 계획하다
arrive 도착하다

# 일반동사의 불규칙 과거형

**A**  Jackson **went** to a party.  잭슨은 파티에 갔다.

**B**  He **wore** a Batman costume.  그는 배트맨 의상을 입었다.

**C**  But the real Batman was there!  하지만 그곳에 진짜 배트맨이 있었다!

### 예문 맛보기

A, B의 went, wore는 각각 go, wear의 과거형이야.

**1**  **불규칙 변화:** 과거형이 −ed로 끝나지 않고 불규칙하게 변하는 동사도 있습니다. 하지만 불규칙하게 변하는 동사들에서도 다음과 같이 약간의 공통점을 찾을 수 있습니다.

**(1) 현재형과 과거형이 같은 동사**

| put − **put** | cut − **cut** | hit − **hit** | read − **read** |
|---|---|---|---|

### Examples

A car **hit** the wall. 자동차 한 대가 벽에 부딪쳤다.
She **read** the letter. 그녀는 그 편지를 읽었다.

**(2) 현재형과 과거형이 다른 동사**

| | | |
|---|---|---|
| sing − **sang** | teach − **taught** | ride − **rode** |
| meet − **met** | catch − **caught** | tell − **told** |
| drink − **drank** | buy − **bought** | sell − **sold** |
| give − **gave** | feel − **felt** | fly − **flew** |
| make − **made** | send − **sent** | know − **knew** |
| come − **came** | sleep − **slept** | grow − **grew** |
| see − **saw** | drive − **drove** | do − **did** |
| wear − **wore** | write − **wrote** | eat − **ate** |
| wake − **woke** | speak − **spoke** | have − **had** |
| swim − **swam** | break − **broke** | go − **went** |

### Examples

I **saw** a monster. 나는 괴물을 보았다.
She **made** some jam. 그녀는 잼을 조금 만들었다.

### BUDDY'S TIPS
표의 각 칸에 제시된 단어들을 여러 번 소리내어 읽어봐. 발음이 비슷하지?

# WARM UP

**A** 다음 중 일반동사의 과거형을 사용한 문장에 ✓ 하세요.

1  Sally knew my secret.  ☐

2  I need new rain boots.  ☐

3  They walk along the river.  ☐

4  A bird sang in the morning.  ☐

5  Ann bought a new camera.  ☐

6  He went to bed early last night.  ☐

Ⓐ
know 알다
secret 비밀
need 필요로 하다
rain boots
장화, 레인 부츠
along …을 따라
early 일찍

**B** 다음 일반동사의 과거형으로 알맞은 것을 고르세요.

| 1 | fly | ① flew | ② flied |
| 2 | tell | ① teld | ② told |
| 3 | drive | ① drove | ② droved |
| 4 | have | ① haved | ② had |
| 5 | sleep | ① slept | ② sleepped |
| 6 | meet | ① melt | ② met |
| 7 | wear | ① weared | ② wore |
| 8 | teach | ① taught | ② teached |

## A 다음 빈칸에 일반동사의 과거형을 쓰세요.

1 hit _____
2 put _____
3 sell _____
4 try _____
5 see _____
6 ride _____
7 have _____
8 dance _____

9 help _____
10 drop _____
11 read _____
12 listen _____
13 speak _____
14 feel _____
15 send _____
16 make _____

A

hit 때리다, 치다
put 놓다, 두다
sell 팔다
try 노력하다
help 돕다
speak 말하다
feel 느끼다
send 보내다
make 만들다

## B ( ) 안에서 알맞은 것을 고르세요.

1 Julie ( studyed / studied ) all day.

2 They ( stoped / stopped ) the game.

3 Jack ( drove / drived ) his car carefully.

4 He ( arrove / arrived ) in Japan yesterday.

5 The duck ( swam / swimmed ) in the pond.

6 My aunt ( worked / workt ) at the bank last year.

7 I ( watchied / watched ) the news last night.

B

all day 하루 종일
stop 멈추다, 중단하다
carefully 조심스럽게
pond 연못

C 우리말과 같은 뜻이 되도록 주어진 단어를 빈칸에 알맞은 형태로 쓰세요.

1 그 소년은 접시들을 깨뜨렸다. (break)

→ The boy _____ the dishes.

2 그들은 버스 정류장에서 만났다. (meet)

→ They _____ at the bus stop.

3 벨라는 가족들과의 여행을 계획했다. (plan)

→ Bella _____ a trip with her family.

4 그녀는 사과를 네 조각으로 잘랐다. (cut)

→ She _____ the apple into four pieces.

C
break 깨뜨리다
dish 접시
bus stop
버스 정류장
trip 여행
cut 자르다
piece 조각

D 다음 그림을 보고 주어진 단어를 이용하여 빈칸에 알맞은 말을 쓰세요.

D
bottle 병
suddenly 갑자기
become …이 되다
next 그 다음에
grow
자라다, *…하게 되다

1 Alice ___saw___ a bottle of juice and a piece of cake. (see)

2 She _____ the juice. (drink)

3 Suddenly, she _____ small. (become)

4 Next, she _____ the cake. (eat)

5 And then, she _____ very large. (grow)

**E** 주어진 단어를 빈칸에 알맞은 형태로 쓰세요.

**1**   wake

I _____ up at seven o'clock every day.

I _____ up at twelve o'clock yesterday.

**2**   have

I _____ spaghetti for lunch every day.

I _____ a salad for lunch yesterday.

**3**   do

I _____ my homework after dinner every day.

I _____ the dishes for my mom yesterday.

**E**
wake up
깨다, 일어나다
spaghetti 스파게티
do one's homework
숙제를 하다
after …뒤에, 후에
do the dishes
설거지를 하다

**F** 다음 일정표를 보고 빈칸에 알맞은 말을 쓰세요.

| Sun | Mon | Tue | Wed | Thu | Fri | Sat |
|-----|-----|-----|-----|-----|-----|-----|
| 19 | 20 | 21 | 22 | 23 | 24 | 25 |
| move to a new house | buy paint and brushes | paint the walls | buy a big sofa | clean the windows | today | |

DECEMBER NOVEMBER OCTOBER SEPTEMBER AUGUST JULY JUNE MAY APRIL MARCH FEBRUARY JANUARY

**1** I _____ last Sunday.

**2** On Tuesday, I _____.

**3** I _____ on Wednesday.

**4** On Thursday, I _____.

**F**
move 이사하다
paint 페인트,
페인트를 칠하다
wall 벽
sofa 소파
clean 청소하다

## A ( ) 안에서 알맞은 것을 고르고, 문장을 우리말로 해석하세요.

1 She ( plantied / **planted** ) a tree last spring.

→ _____

2 He ( wears / wore ) a blue sweater yesterday.

→ _____

3 They ( used / use ) your computer yesterday.

→ _____

4 She ( goed / went ) to the coffee shop last night.

→ _____

## B 다음 문장에서 틀린 부분을 고쳐 문장을 다시 쓰세요.

1 I catched the ball.

→ _____

2 She putted her bag on the chair.

→ _____

3 The baby cryed very loudly.

→ _____

4 Albert teached English at school in 2012.

→ _____

5 My teacher gived homework to us last class.

→ _____

*Vocabulary*

**A**
plant
(나무 등을) 심다
spring 봄
use 사용하다, 쓰다

**B**
catch 잡다
loudly 큰 소리로
give 주다
class 수업

일반동사의 과거형 1 ▪ **39**

# 재미있는 동물 이야기

난 엘리베이터 타고 간다!

앗, 잠시만요!

모기는 아파트 몇 층까지 올라갈 수 있을까요? 모기가 한 번에 올라갈 수 있는 높이는 약 20m, 즉 아파트 5~6층 높이입니다. 하지만 사람들처럼 엘리베이터를 통해서 올라가기도 해서 아주 높은 층까지도 갈 수 있어요.

너도 7개?!

사람과 기린의 목뼈의 개수는 같아요. 둘 다 일곱 개의 목뼈를 가지고 있어요.

벌이 춤을 추는 이유는 동료들에게 꿀의 위치를 알리기 위해서 입니다. 꿀이 90m 이내에 있을 때는 O자 춤을, 그것보다 멀리 있을 때는 8자 춤을 춥니다.

아따 조용하네~

뱀에게는 귀가 없어서 소리를 들을 수 없어요. 대신 땅의 진동을 통해 누가 접근하는지 알 수 있다고 합니다.

**UNIT 04** 일반동사의 과거형 2: 부정문과 의문문

## 다시 보기

지난 Unit에서 배운 내용을 다시 확인해 보세요.

☆ **일반동사의 과거형 (규칙 변화)**

| | | | |
|---|---|---|---|
| call – call**ed** | love – love**d** | try – tr**ied** | plan – plan**ned** |
| visit – visit**ed** | arrive – arrive**d** | cry – cr**ied** | drop – drop**ped** |

☆ **일반동사의 과거형 (불규칙 변화)**

| | | | |
|---|---|---|---|
| put – **put** | make – **made** | teach – **taught** | go – **went** |
| sing – **sang** | write – **wrote** | know – **knew** | eat – **ate** |
| tell – **told** | wear – **wore** | come – **came** | do – **did** |

## 미리 보기

만화를 통해 이번 Unit에서 배울 내용을 미리 살펴보세요.

# 부정문 만들기: 일반동사의 과거형

**A** Today was a terrible day.  오늘은 끔찍한 날이었다.

**B** I **didn't bring** my homework.  나는 숙제를 가져오지 않았다.

**C** I **didn't take** my umbrella.  나는 우산을 들고 오지 않았다.

**D** I **didn't have** my key.  나는 열쇠를 가지고 있지 않았다.

### 예문 맛보기

B, C, D에서 동사 앞에 didn't가 쓰인 이유는 무엇일까?

**1** 일반동사 과거형의 부정문은 did not을 사용하여 만듭니다. 「**주어+did not+동사원형** …」의 형태로 쓰며, '**…하지 않았다**'라고 해석합니다. 이때 did는 주어에 상관없이 항상 같은 형태로 사용합니다.

I lied. 나는 거짓말을 했다.

I **did not** lie. 나는 거짓말을 하지 않았다.

He played the piano. 그는 피아노를 쳤다.

He **did not** play the piano. 그는 피아노를 치지 않았다.

### Examples

I **did not forget** you. 나는 너를 잊지 않았다.

You **did not listen** to me. 너는 내 말을 듣지 않았다.

They **did not know** each other. 그들은 서로 몰랐다.

The baby **did not cry** last night. 그 아기는 지난밤에 울지 않았다.

> 기억나!
> 일반동사 현재형의 부정문은 did 대신에 do/does를 넣어주면 돼.
> 「주어+do/does not+동사원형 …」

**2** did not은 **didn't**로 줄여 쓸 수 있습니다.

### Examples

I **didn't kick** the ball. 나는 공을 발로 차지 않았다.

We **didn't go** to the sea. 우리는 바다에 가지 않았다.

They **didn't have** lunch. 그들은 점심을 먹지 않았다.

Juliet **didn't wait** for Romeo. 줄리엣은 로미오를 기다리지 않았다.

**CHECK UP**

다음 문장에서 did not이 들어갈 위치에 ✓ 하세요.

1 She ① look ② at ③ him.

2 My ① cat ② sleep ③ last night.

3 Cinderella ① like ② her ③ sisters.

# WARM UP

**A** 다음 중 일반동사 과거형의 부정문에 ✓ 하세요.

1 I don't lie. ☐

2 I kicked the ball. ☐

3 We did not go to the sea. ☐

4 They had lunch together. ☐

5 You did not wait for me. ☐

6 Janet doesn't brush her hair. ☐

7 I didn't understand the book. ☐

8 Michael didn't swim in the pool. ☐

Ⓐ
lie 거짓말하다
kick (발로) 차다
sea 바다
together 함께
wait 기다리다
brush one's hair
머리를 빗다
understand
이해하다
swim 수영하다
pool 수영장

**B** 다음 문장의 밑줄 친 부분을 줄임형으로 쓰세요.

1 He <u>did not have</u> a car. → _____

2 I <u>did not eat</u> your toast. → _____

3 The horse <u>did not run</u> fast. → _____

4 Miranda <u>did not like</u> cucumbers. → _____

5 They <u>did not know</u> each other. → _____

6 We <u>did not use</u> our phones in class. → _____

Ⓑ
toast 토스트
fast 빨리, 빠르게
cucumber 오이
know 알다
each other 서로
use 사용하다

# 의문문 만들기: 일반동사의 과거형

**A** **Did** you **watch** the movie?   너 그 영화 봤니?

**B** **Yes**, I **did.**   응, 봤어.

**C** **Did** you **like** it?   좋았니?

**D** **No**, I **didn't.** It was boring.   아니, 좋지 않았어. 그건 지루했어.

### 예문 맛보기

일반동사로 과거의 일을 묻거나 답할 때도 did가 필요해!

**1** 일반동사 과거형의 의문문은 did를 맨 앞에 써서 「**Did + 주어 + 동사원형 …?**」의 형태로 쓰고, '**…했니?**'라고 해석합니다.

**You heard** the news. 너는 그 소식을 들었다.      **He laughed** loudly. 그는 크게 웃었다.

**Did you hear** the news? 너 그 소식 들었니?      **Did he laugh** loudly? 그는 크게 웃었니?

### Examples

**Did** he **buy** the bicycle? 그가 그 자전거를 샀니?
**Did** Dustin **win** the game? 더스틴이 게임에서 이겼니?
**Did** you **finish** the homework? 너는 숙제를 다 끝냈니?
**Did** the guests **like** my food? 손님들이 내 음식을 좋아했니?

> 기억나?!
> 일반동사 현재형의
> 의문문은 Did 대신에 Do/Does를
> 넣어주면 돼.
> 「Do/Does + 주어 + 동사원형 …?」

**2** 일반동사 과거형의 의문문에는 다음과 같이 대답합니다.

| 긍정 대답 | 부정 대답 |
|---|---|
| **Yes**, 주어 + **did.** | **No**, 주어 + **didn't.** |

### Examples

A: Did you bring an umbrella? 너는 우산을 가져왔니?
B: **Yes**, I **did.** 응, 가져왔어. / **No**, I **didn't.** 아니, 안 가져왔어.

A: Did they play the song? 그들이 그 노래를 연주했니?
B: **Yes**, they **did.** 응, 연주했어. / **No**, they **didn't.** 아니, 연주하지 않았어.

### CHECK UP

다음 우리말과 같은 뜻이 되도록 빈칸에 알맞은 말을 쓰세요.

**1** 너는 네이트를 봤니?          → _____ you see Nate?

**2** 너는 비밀번호를 잊어버렸니?  → _____ you forget the password?

**3** 그녀가 너를 파티에 초대했니?  → _____ she invite you to the party?

# WARM UP

Vocabulary

 다음 중 일반동사 과거형의 의문문에 ✓ 하세요.

1  Did you live in Canada? ☐

2  Did Julie plant the trees? ☐

3  Did he bring his girlfriend? ☐

4  Does the sun set in the west? ☐

5  Did they play hockey in school? ☐

6  Do you sleep late on Sundays? ☐

7  Does your mom work at a hospital? ☐

A
Canada 캐나다
bring 데려오다
girlfriend 여자 친구
set (해·달이) 지다
west 서쪽
hockey 하키
late 늦게

B  ( ) 안에서 알맞은 것을 고르세요.

1  A: Did you wear a hat?
   B: No, I ( did / didn't ).

2  A: Did he like your gift?
   B: Yes, he ( did / didn't ).

3  A: Did she find her wallet?
   B: No, she ( did / didn't ).

4  A: Did you exercise yesterday?
   B: No, I ( did / didn't ).

5  A: Did Bob paint this picture?
   B: Yes, he ( did / didn't ).

B
find 찾다
wallet 지갑
exercise 운동하다

##  A ( ) 안에서 알맞은 것을 고르세요.

1 She didn't ( buy / buys ) the skirt.

2 Did Nick ( go / goes ) to the park?

3 I ( didn't / don't ) sleep last night.

4 We didn't ( miss / missed ) the bus.

5 Did Britney ( finish / finished ) her work?

6 ( Did / Does ) you see the rainbow this morning?

##  B 다음 우리말과 같은 뜻이 되도록 〈보기〉의 단어를 이용하여 문장을 완성하세요.

| 〈보기〉 | meet | wear | drink | write |

1 그녀는 그 우유를 마시지 않았다.

→ She _____ _____ the milk.

2 그들은 어제 만나지 않았다.

→ They _____ _____ yesterday.

3 나는 그에게 편지를 쓰지 않았다.

→ I _____ _____ a letter to him.

4 제시는 그 셔츠를 다시 입지 않았다.

→ Jessy _____ _____ the shirt again.

**Vocabulary**

A
buy 사다
park 공원
miss 놓치다
finish 끝내다
rainbow 무지개

B
wear 입다
drink 마시다
again 다시

C 주어진 단어를 이용하여 빈칸에 알맞은 말을 쓰세요.

1 _____ he _____ for you last night? (wait)

2 _____ they _____ yesterday? (study)

3 _____ the World Cup _____ in 1930?
(start)

4 _____ you _____ for dinner last night?
(pay)

Vocabulary

C
start 시작하다
pay 지불하다

D 다음 그림을 보고 주어진 단어를 이용하여 빈칸에 알맞은 말을 쓰세요.

1
ride

2
eat

3
stay

D
go fishing
낚시를 가다
motorcycle
오토바이
tent 텐트

My father and uncle went fishing last weekend.

1 They _____ _____ bicycles.

They _____ motorcycles.

2 They _____ _____ meat.

They _____ fish.

3 They _____ _____ in a hotel.

They _____ in a tent.

E 다음 그림을 보고 주어진 단어를 이용하여 빈칸에 알맞은 말을 쓰세요.

1 A: ___Did___ Mary ___wear___ a black dress? (wear)

  B: ___Yes___ , ___she___ ___did___ .

2 A: _____ David _____ dinner alone? (have)

  B: _____ , _____ _____ .

3 A: _____ Paul _____ the food? (serve)

  B: _____ , _____ _____ .

4 A: _____ Olivia and Jane _____ pasta? (eat)

  B: _____ , _____ _____ .

F 다음 문장에서 밑줄 친 부분을 바르게 고쳐 쓰세요.

F
brush one's teeth
양치질하다
market 시장
answer the phone
전화를 받다

1 Did he <u>buys</u> oranges?　　　→ _____

2 Larry didn't <u>brushed</u> his teeth.　　→ _____

3 She didn't <u>goes</u> to the market.　　→ _____

4 Did Debbie <u>answered</u> the phone?　→ _____

 다음 문장을 (   ) 안의 지시대로 바꿔 쓰세요.

**1** He walked the dog. (의문문)

→ _____

**2** Ken enjoyed the game. (부정문)

→ _____

**3** She took off her mask. (의문문)

→ _____

**4** I drank coffee this morning. (부정문)

→ _____

**5** The runner finished the race. (부정문)

→ _____

Ⓐ
walk a dog
개를 산책시키다
enjoy 즐기다
game 게임, 경기
take off 벗다
mask 가면
runner
(경주에 참석한) 주자
race 경주

Ⓑ 주어진 말을 이용하여 우리말에 맞게 영작하세요.

**1** 그들은 인도를 여행했니? (they, travel to India)

→ _____

**2** 그는 설거지를 하지 않았다. (he, do the dishes)

→ _____

**3** 그녀가 내 피자를 먹었니? (she, eat my pizza)

→ _____

**4** 나는 그 창문을 깨지 않았다. (I, break the window)

→ _____

Ⓑ
travel 여행하다
India 인도
break 깨다

# UNIT 03~04
# REVIEW TEST

[1–3] 다음 중 동사의 과거형이 잘못 연결된 것을 고르세요.

**1**
① cry – cried
② love – loved
③ grow – grew
④ drop – droped

**2**
① tell – told
② make – maked
③ wake – woke
④ open – opened

**3**
① eat – eat
② put – put
③ go – went
④ have – had

**4** 빈칸에 알맞은 말을 쓰세요.

_____ you sleep well last night?

[5–6] 빈칸에 들어갈 수 없는 것을 고르세요.

**5**
Daniel did not _____ it.

① cut
② see
③ knew
④ believe

**6**
I _____ my car last month.

① sell
② drove
③ bought
④ washed

**7** 다음 질문에 대한 대답으로 알맞은 것을 고르세요.

Did Peter and Susan meet at the library?

① No, they don't.
② Yes, they were.
③ No, they didn't.
④ No, they weren't.

**8** 빈칸에 들어갈 말이 바르게 짝지어진 것을 고르세요.

> The woman didn't _____ jeans. She _____ a skirt yesterday.

① wear – wears    ② wear – wore

③ wore – wears    ④ wore – wore

**9** 다음 문장을 의문문으로 바르게 바꾼 것을 고르세요.

> Lisa changed her clothes.

① Did Lisa change her clothes?

② Does Lisa change her clothes?

③ Did Lisa changed her clothes?

④ Does Lisa changed her clothes?

[10-11] 다음 중 틀린 문장을 고르세요.

**10** ① I smelled the flower.

② Ron did his homework.

③ We helped our teacher.

④ The king did lived in the castle.

**11** ① The bug didn't move.

② Charles read the memo.

③ Did Harry drinks the tea?

④ He didn't spend the money.

**12** 다음 우리말을 영어로 바르게 옮긴 것을 고르세요.

> 엘사는 여름을 좋아하지 않았다.

① Elsa not liked summer.

② Elsa did not like summer.

③ Elsa does not like summer.

④ Elsa was not like summer.

**13** 빈칸에 알맞은 말을 쓰세요.

> A: Did David draw the picture?
> B: Yes, _____ _____.

**14** 다음 문장을 과거시제로 바꿀 때 빈칸에 알맞은 말을 쓰세요.

> My neighbor has a dog.

→ My neighbor _____ a dog.

**15** 다음 문장에서 틀린 부분을 찾아 바르게 고쳐 쓰세요.

> They move to Seoul in 2006.

_____ → _____

# 풀어봐, 넌센스 퀴즈!

1. 오이가 무를 때렸다를 네 글자로 줄이면?

2. 실내화가 자기소개를 할 때 뭐라고 할까?

3. 버스에 노인이 아무리 많아도 항상 앉아서 가는 사람은?

4. 반성문을 영어로 하면?

5. 모든 사람들을 일으킬 수 있는 숫자는?

공오이무

실내에요인가

운전기사

미안

하나둘셋

# 현재진행형

## 다시 보기

지난 Unit에서 배운 내용을 다시 확인해 보세요.

### ☆ 일반동사 과거형의 부정문

I **did not forget** you. 나는 너를 잊지 않았다.

You **did not listen** to me. 너는 내 말을 듣지 않았다.

They **didn't have** lunch. 그들은 점심을 먹지 않았다.

Juliet **didn't wait** for Romeo. 줄리엣은 로미오를 기다리지 않았다.

### ☆ 일반동사 과거형의 의문문

A: **Did** you **bring** an umbrella? 너는 우산을 가져왔니?

B: **Yes**, I **did**. 응, 가져왔어. / **No**, I **didn't**. 아니, 안 가져왔어.

A: **Did** they **play** the song? 그들이 그 노래를 연주했니?

B: **Yes**, they **did**. 응, 연주했어. / **No**, they **didn't**. 아니, 연주하지 않았어.

## 미리 보기

만화를 통해 이번 Unit에서 배울 내용을 미리 살펴보세요.

# 현재진행형의 의미와 형태

**A** Today is Christmas Eve.  오늘은 크리스마스 이브이다.

**B** I **am decorating** the tree.  나는 트리를 장식하고 있다.

**C** It is very fun.  그것은 정말 재미있다.

**예문 맛보기**

B의 am decorating은 어떤 의미일까?

**1** 현재진행형은 **지금 진행 중인 일**을 나타낼 때 사용합니다. 현재진행형 문장에서는 동사를 「**be동사+동사원형-ing**」의 형태로 쓰며, '**…하고 있다**'라고 해석합니다.

### Examples

I **am reading** a magazine. 나는 잡지를 읽고 있다.
He **is going** to the gym. 그는 체육관에 가고 있다.
A man **is taking** a picture. 한 남자가 사진을 찍고 있다.
People **are running** for the bus. 사람들이 버스를 향해 달려가고 있다.

> **BUDDY'S TIPS**
> 현재진행형에서 be동사는 주어의 인칭과 수에 따라 am, are, is 중 알맞은 것을 쓰면 돼.

**2** 현재진행형에서 동사원형에 -ing를 붙이는 방법은 다음과 같습니다.

| 동사의 형태 | 규칙 | Examples | |
|---|---|---|---|
| 대부분의 동사 | 동사원형+-ing | watch – watch**ing**  clean – clean**ing** | do – do**ing**  drink – drink**ing** |
| -e로 끝나는 동사 | e를 빼고+-ing | dance – danc**ing**  write – writ**ing** | bake – bak**ing**  make – mak**ing** |
| -ie로 끝나는 동사 | ie를 y로 고치고+-ing | die – d**ying**  lie – l**ying** | tie – t**ying** |
| 「단모음+단자음」으로 끝나는 동사 | 맨 뒤 자음을 한 번 더 쓰고+-ing | stop – stop**ping**  cut – cut**ting** | run – run**ning**  swim – swim**ming** |

### Examples

I **am writing** an e-mail. 나는 이메일을 쓰고 있다.
She **is tying** a ribbon. 그녀는 리본을 묶고 있다.
Sam **is cutting** the rope. 샘은 그 밧줄을 자르고 있다.
Andy **is watching** TV. 앤디는 TV를 보고 있다.

# WARM UP

**Vocabulary**

Ⓐ
bake 굽다
clean 청소하다

Ⓐ 다음 우리말과 일치하는 문장을 고르세요.

1 앨리스는 자고 있다.
  a Alice sleeps.
  b Alice is sleeping.

2 로빈은 우유를 마시고 있다.
  a Robin drinks milk.
  b Robin is drinking milk.

3 나는 쿠키를 굽고 있다.
  a I am baking cookies.
  b I is baking cookies.

4 그녀는 그 방을 청소하고 있다.
  a She cleans the room.
  b She is cleaning the room.

Ⓑ 다음 동사의 「동사원형-ing」 형태로 알맞은 것을 고르세요.

Ⓑ
die 죽다
cut 자르다
stop 멈추다

1 die      ( dieing / dying )

2 do      ( doing / dooing )

3 cut      ( cuting / cutting )

4 write      ( writing / writting )

5 stop      ( stoping / stopping )

6 dance      ( dancing / danceing )

7 read      ( reading / readding )

# 부정문과 의문문 만들기: 현재진행형

A   You are drawing a picture.   너 그림 그리고 있구나.

B   Is it a monkey?   그거 원숭이야?

C   I **am not drawing** a monkey.   난 원숭이를 그리고 있지 않아.

D   I am drawing you.   나는 너를 그리고 있어.

### 예문 맛보기

C에서 not의 위치를 확인해 보자!

**1** 현재진행형의 부정형은 be동사에 뒤에 not을 붙인 「**be동사+not+동사원형-ing**」의 형태로, '…**하고 있지 않다**'라는 의미입니다.

Emma is singing. → Emma is ‿^not‿ singing.
엠마는 노래하고 있다.       엠마는 노래하고 있지 않다.

> 「be동사+not」이나
> 「대명사 주어+be동사」는 줄여 쓸
> 수 있어.
> You are not singing.
> = You aren't singing.
> = You're not singing.
> 너는 노래하고 있지 않다.

### Examples

I **am not reading** a book. 나는 책을 읽고 있지 않다.
We **are not walking**. 우리는 걷고 있지 않다.
She **isn't eating** a sandwich. 그녀는 샌드위치를 먹고 있지 않다.
They**'re not playing** soccer. 그들은 축구를 하고 있지 않다.

**2** 현재진행형의 의문문은 be동사와 주어의 위치를 바꾼 「**be동사+주어+동사원형-ing** …?」의 형태로, '…**하고 있니?**'라는 의미입니다. 이에 대한 긍정 대답은 「**Yes, 주어+be동사.**」, 부정 대답은 「**No, 주어 +be동사+not.**」으로 합니다.

### Examples

A: **Is** he **riding** a bicycle? 그는 자전거를 타고 있니?
B: **Yes**, he **is**. 응, 타고 있어. / **No**, he **isn't**. 아니, 타고 있지 않아.

A: **Are** the dogs **sleeping**? 그 개들은 자고 있니?
B: **Yes**, they **are**. 응, 자고 있어. / **No**, they **aren't**. 아니, 자고 있지 않아.

### PLUS 진행형으로 쓰지 않는 동사

동작이 아닌 지속적인 상태를 나타내는 동사는 진행형으로 쓰지 않습니다.

like 좋아하다   have 가지다   know 알다   want 원하다   need 필요로 하다

I am liking pizza. (X)        I like pizza. (O) 나는 피자를 좋아한다.
I am having a pencil. (X)     I have a pencil. (O) 나는 연필 한 자루를 가지고 있다.

# WARM UP

**Vocabulary**

Ⓐ
paint 페인트칠하다
ceiling 천장
listen 듣다
loudly 큰 소리로

Ⓐ 다음 문장에서 not이 들어갈 위치에 ✓ 하세요.

1 I ① am ② writing ③ a letter.

2 The ① babies ② are ③ crying.

3 Tony ① is ② learning ③ English.

4 He ① is ② painting ③ the ceiling.

5 They're ① listening ② to ③ music.

6 She ① is ② eating ③ ice cream.

7 My ① friends ② are ③ singing loudly.

Ⓑ 다음 중 현재진행형의 의문문을 고르세요.

Ⓑ
handsome
멋진, 잘생긴
noisy 시끄러운
sit 앉다

1 Is Luke handsome? ☐

2 Is he sleeping now? ☐

3 Is Tiffany wearing a skirt? ☐

4 Does Jack like melons? ☐

5 Were the children noisy? ☐

6 Are you riding a bicycle? ☐

7 Are the girls sitting on the chairs? ☐

## A  ( ) 안에서 알맞은 것을 고르세요.

1  Patrick is ( play / playing ) guitar.

2  I ( need / am needing ) an empty box.

3  Is Jack ( helping / help ) his mother now?

4  They are ( talk / talking ) about the movie.

5  Ducks are ( swiming / swimming ) in the lake.

6  She is ( speaking not / not speaking ) in Korean.

7  ( Are they / They are ) doing their homework?

**Vocabulary**

**A**
need 필요로 하다
empty 비어 있는, 빈
talk 이야기하다
duck 오리
lake 호수
Korean 한국어

## B  다음 동사를 「동사원형-ing」 형태로 쓰세요.

1  tie _____        7  make _____

2  drop _____      8  bake _____

3  kick _____       9  use _____

4  tell _____       10  run _____

5  rain _____      11  fly _____

6  touch _____    12  write _____

**B**
tie 묶다, 매다
drop 떨어뜨리다
kick (발로) 차다
touch 만지다

C 우리말과 같은 뜻이 되도록 주어진 단어를 이용하여 문장을 완성하세요.

1 그는 샤워를 하고 있니? (take)
→ _____ _____ _____ a shower?

2 그들은 옷을 사고 있지 않다. (buy)
→ They _____ _____ clothes.

3 우리는 산에 오르고 있다. (climb)
→ We _____ _____ a mountain.

4 농부가 돼지들에게 먹이를 주고 있다. (feed)
→ A farmer _____ _____ the pigs.

C
take a shower
샤워를 하다
climb
오르다, 올라가다
mountain 산
feed 먹이를 주다
farmer 농부

D 다음 그림을 보고 〈보기〉의 단어와 현재진행형을 이용하여 문장을 완성하세요.

D
skate
스케이트를 타다
hold 들고 있다

〈보기〉   watch        skate        hold        dance

1

Yuna _____ _____
on the ice.

2

They _____ _____
the baseball game.

3

She _____ _____
on the stage.

4

I _____ _____ a
book.

**E** 주어진 단어와 현재진행형을 이용하여 빈칸에 알맞은 말을 쓰세요.

**1** A: _____ Julie _____? (smile)

B: Yes, _____ _____.

**2** A: _____ he _____ the ball? (throw)

B: No, _____ _____.

**3** A: _____ they _____ on the beach? (lie)

B: Yes, _____ _____.

**4** A: _____ you _____ to the radio? (listen)

B: Yes, _____ _____.

**F** 다음 그림을 보고 주어진 단어와 현재진행형을 이용하여 빈칸에 알맞은 말을 쓰세요.

**1** A girl _____ a red hood. (wear)

**2** She _____ on the door. (knock)

**3** A wolf _____ inside. (wait)

**4** He _____. (sleep)

*Vocabulary*

**E**
smile 웃다, 미소짓다
throw 던지다
beach 해변
lie 누워 있다

**F**
hood
(외투 등에 달린) 모자
knock
노크하다, 두드리다
inside 안에
wait 기다리다

*Vocabulary*

Ⓐ
dry one's hair
머리를 말리다
fly 날리다, 날다
kite 연
fix 고치다

Ⓐ 다음 우리말과 같은 뜻이 되도록 (  ) 안의 말을 바르게 배열하세요.

**1** 나의 엄마가 케이크를 자르고 있다.
(cutting / the cake / is / my mom)

→ _____

**2** 티파니는 그녀의 머리를 말리고 있다.
(is / her hair / Tiffany / drying)

→ _____

**3** 우리는 연을 날리고 있지 않다.
(not / we / flying a kite / are)

→ _____

**4** 그들은 차를 고치고 있니?
(fixing / they / are / the car)

→ _____

Ⓑ 주어진 말을 이용하여 우리말에 맞게 영작하세요.

**1** 나뭇잎들이 떨어지고 있다. (leaves, fall)

→ _____

**2** 비행기가 착륙하고 있다. (the plane, land)

→ _____

**3** 그들은 테니스를 치고 있지 않다. (they, play tennis)

→ _____

**4** 그녀는 집에 가고 있니? (she, go home)

→ _____

# 디디를 찾아라!

안녕? 내 어항을 구경해 봐. 물고기들이 귀엽지?
이 중에서 내가 가장 좋아하는 물고기 "디디"를 찾아봐.

힌트
1. 디디는 노란색이 들어간 물고기야.
2. 디디의 꼬리는 노란색이 아니야.
3. 디디는 줄무늬가 있어.
4. 디디는 날카로운 이빨이 없어.
5. 디디는 어항에서 가장 큰 물고기가 아니야.

# UNIT 06 형용사

## 다시 보기

지난 Unit에서 배운 내용을 다시 확인해 보세요.

### ☆ 현재진행형

I **am reading** a magazine. 나는 잡지를 읽고 있다.
People **are running** for the bus. 사람들이 버스를 향해 달려가고 있다.

### ☆ 현재진행형의 부정문

We **are not walking**. 우리는 걷고 있지 않다.
She **isn't eating** a sandwich. 그녀는 샌드위치를 먹고 있지 않다.
They**'re not playing** soccer. 그들은 축구를 하고 있지 않다.

### ☆ 현재진행형의 의문문

A: **Is** he **riding** a bicycle? 그는 자전거를 타고 있니?
B: **Yes**, he **is**. 응, 타고 있어. / **No**, he **isn't**. 아니, 타고 있지 않아.

## 미리 보기

만화를 통해 이번 Unit에서 배울 내용을 미리 살펴보세요.

# 형용사의 종류와 역할

**A** Olly is a snowman.  올리는 눈사람이다.

**B** He is **white**.  그는 하얗다.

**C** He has **short** arms.  그는 짧은 팔을 가지고 있다.

**D** He hates **sunny** days.  그는 화창한 날을 싫어한다.

### 예문 맛보기
B의 white, C의 short, D의 sunny는 모두 형용사야.

**1** **형용사**는 **명사의 생김새**나 **기분, 상태** 등을 구체적으로 설명해 주는 말입니다. 우리말로는 '큰', '행복한', '아픈' 같은 말들이 바로 형용사입니다. 형용사는 주로 '···**인**', '···**한**'이라고 해석합니다.

| 크기 · 모양 | big 큰   small 작은   short 키가 작은   round 둥근 |
|---|---|
| 색깔 | red 빨간   blue 파란   yellow 노란   white 흰 |
| 기분 · 성격 | happy 행복한   sad 슬픈   angry 화난   kind 친절한 |
| 상태 | good 좋은   new 새로운   old 늙은   beautiful 아름다운 |
| 날씨 | sunny 화창한   rainy 비가 오는   windy 바람 부는   warm 따뜻한 |

**2** 형용사는 **명사의 앞**에서 명사를 구체적으로 설명해 줍니다. 이때 형용사는 a/an이나 the와 같은 관사나 my, his와 같은 소유격 뒤에 위치합니다.

James drives a **blue** car. 제임스는 파란 자동차를 운전한다.

### Examples
John likes his **new** bag. 존은 그의 새 가방을 좋아한다.
The bird caught a **small** fish. 그 새는 작은 물고기를 잡았다.

> **기억나!**
> 명사란 Elsa(엘사),
> bed(침대)처럼 사람이나 사물의
> 이름을 나타내는 말이야.

**3** 형용사는 **동사의 뒤**에서 주어를 보충 설명하기도 합니다.

The table is **round**. 그 테이블은 둥글다.

### Examples
The paintings are **beautiful**. 그 그림들은 아름답다.
The soup looks **delicious**. 그 수프는 맛있어 보인다.

# WARM UP

**A** ( ) 안에서 형용사를 고르고, 우리말 뜻을 쓰세요.

1 ( rose / red ) _____

2 ( look / round ) _____

3 ( they / happy ) _____

4 ( drive / sunny ) _____

5 ( have / good ) _____

6 ( angry / mouth ) _____

7 ( smell / yellow ) _____

8 ( today / small ) _____

**B** 다음 문장에서 형용사에 밑줄을 긋고, 그것이 설명하는 말에 O 하세요.

1 This is a big table.

2 My mom is beautiful.

3 I ate a sweet peach.

4 There is a white dress.

5 The weather is cold.

6 It is my new hairband.

7 The movie is interesting.

**B**
peach 복숭아
weather 날씨
cold 추운, 차가운
hairband 머리띠
interesting
재미있는

# 수와 양을 나타내는 형용사

**A** **Some** boys read books.  몇몇 소년들은 책을 읽는다.

**B** **Some** girls talk loudly.  몇몇 소녀들은 시끄럽게 얘기를 한다.

**C** They don't drink **any** coffee!  그들은 어떤 커피도 마시지 않는다!

### 예문 맛보기

some과 any도 형용사야. 이 단어들은 어떻게 쓰는 걸까?

**1** **some**은 '약간의', '몇몇의'라는 뜻으로 주로 **긍정문**에서 쓰입니다.

### Examples

I baked **some** cookies. 나는 쿠키를 몇 개 구웠다.
Toby has **some** coins. 토비는 동전 몇 개를 가지고 있다.
There is **some** milk. 우유가 약간 있다.

**2** **any**는 '약간의 …도'라는 뜻으로 주로 **부정문과 의문문**에서 쓰입니다. 부정문에서는 '조금도/전혀(…이 없다)'라고 해석합니다.

### Examples

I don't need **any** help. 나는 도움이 조금도 필요 없다.
He doesn't have **any** friends. 그는 친구가 전혀 없다.
Is there **any** problem? 무슨 문제가 있니?

> **BUDDY'S TIPS**
> some과 any는 셀 수 있는 명사와
> 셀 수 없는 명사 앞에 모두 쓸 수 있어.

**3** **many**와 **much**는 둘 다 '**많은**'이라는 뜻입니다. many는 **셀 수 있는 명사** 앞에, much는 **셀 수 없는 명사** 앞에 쓰입니다.

### Examples

The bug has **many** legs. 그 벌레는 다리가 많다.
There are **many** books on the shelf. 책꽂이에 많은 책이 있다.

We don't have **much** time. 우리에게는 시간이 많이 없다.
Camels don't drink **much** water. 낙타는 물을 많이 마시지 않는다.

**4** **a lot of**와 **lots of**도 '**많은**'이라는 뜻으로, 셀 수 있는 명사와 셀 수 없는 명사 앞에 **모두** 쓸 수 있습니다.

### Examples

**A lot of** people laughed. 많은 사람들이 웃었다.
Bill has **lots of** money. 빌은 많은 돈을 가지고 있다.

# WARM UP

**A** 다음 문장에서 수와 양을 나타내는 형용사에 ○ 하세요.

1 Toby has some coins.

2 He doesn't eat any fish.

3 We wasted a lot of time.

4 Do you have any questions?

5 Lots of hotels have free Internet.

6 There are many cars on the road.

7 There isn't much juice in the cup.

**B** 다음 빈칸에 들어갈 말로 알맞은 것을 모두 고르세요.

| | | | |
|---|---|---|---|
| 1 _____ lions | a many | b much | |
| 2 _____ meat | a much | b a lot of | |
| 3 _____ time | a many | b much | |
| 4 _____ salt | a many | b much | |
| 5 _____ water | a much | b a lot of | |
| 6 _____ pants | a many | b lots of | |
| 7 _____ countries | a many | b much | |

**A** ( ) 안에서 알맞은 것을 고르세요.

1 My grandfather ( is old / old is ).

2 I have ( much / lots of ) comic books.

3 There was too ( much / many ) noise.

4 The baby knows ( many / much ) words.

5 This is an ( expensive bag / bag expensive ).

6 There is ( some / any ) milk in the bottle.

7 There aren't ( some / any ) sheep on the farm.

**B** 다음 문장에서 주어진 형용사가 들어갈 위치에 ✓ 하세요.

1 spicy    Peppers ① are ②.

2 many    I ① need ② pencils.

3 new    He ① lost ② his ③ cell phone.

4 white    I'm ① wearing ② a ③ jacket.

5 much    She ① doesn't ② have ③ time.

6 some    The magician ① showed ② cards.

7 any    There ① aren't ② eggs ③ in the basket.

*Vocabulary*

**A**
noise 소리, 소음
word 단어, 낱말
expensive 비싼
bottle 병
sheep 양
farm 농장

**B**
spicy 향이 강한
pepper 후추
lose 잃어버리다
cell phone 휴대폰
jacket 재킷, 상의
magician 마술사
show 보여주다
basket 바구니

C 다음 그림을 보고 주어진 단어를 이용하여 문장을 완성하세요.

C
full 가득한
empty 비어 있는
round 둥근
square
정사각형 모양의
bowl 그릇, 통

1  2  3

long / short    full / empty    round / square

1 The girl has _____ hair.

The boy has _____ hair.

2 The bowl is _____.

The cup is _____.

3 His glasses are _____.

Her glasses are _____.

D 다음 우리말과 같은 뜻이 되도록 빈칸에 some이나 any 중 알맞은 것을 쓰세요.

1 그들에게는 자녀들이 몇 명 있다.

→ They have _____ children.

2 그녀는 채소를 전혀 먹지 않았다.

→ She didn't eat _____ vegetables.

3 바다에 상어들이 몇 마리 있다.

→ There are _____ sharks in the sea.

4 병 안에 잼이 조금도 없었다.

→ There wasn't _____ jam in the jar.

**E** 다음 문장과 같은 뜻이 되도록 빈칸에 many나 much 중 알맞은 것을 쓰세요.

**1** We have a lot of homework.

→ We have _____ homework.

**2** There isn't a lot of air in the balloon.

→ There isn't _____ air in the balloon.

**3** They planted a lot of trees in the garden.

→ They planted _____ trees in the garden.

**4** There were a lot of candles in the room.

→ There were _____ candles in the room.

**F** 그림을 보고 주어진 말과 〈보기〉의 단어를 이용하여 문장을 완성하세요.

| 〈보기〉 | yellow | blue | any | some |

**1** Amy is wearing a _____. (shirt)

**2** She is riding a _____. (bicycle)

**3** She has _____ in her basket. (books)

**4** There aren't _____ in the sky. (birds)

**Vocabulary**

**E**
homework 숙제
air 공기
balloon 풍선
plant (나무 등을) 심다
garden 뜰, 정원
candle 양초

**F**
ride 타다

 ( ) 안의 말을 바르게 배열하여 문장을 완성하세요.

1 우리는 기름이 많이 필요하다. (oil / need / we / a lot of)

→ _____

2 그것은 지루한 게임이었다. (boring / a / game / was / that)

→ _____

3 그 소녀는 친절하고 예쁘다.
(kind / the girl / and / is / pretty)

→ _____

4 나의 코트에는 단추가 많다.
( my / coat / buttons / has / many)

→ _____

5 그 검은 가방은 비싸다.
(bag / is / black / expensive / the)

→ _____

B 다음 문장에서 <u>틀린</u> 부분을 찾아 바르게 고쳐 쓰세요.

1 Liam absent is.

2 I like new my bedroom.

3 He wanted a blanket warm.

4 They took much pictures in Italy.

5 There isn't many water in the bath.

6 She bought any lemons for lemonade.

**1** 「동사원형-ing」 형태가 <u>잘못</u> 연결된 것을 고르세요.

① die – dying

② run – runing

③ think – thinking

④ make – making

**2** 형용사가 <u>아닌</u> 것을 고르세요.

① sick      ② deep

③ quiet      ④ hobby

[3-4] 빈칸에 들어갈 말로 알맞은 것을 고르세요.

**3** I put _____ on the desk.

① heavy my bag

② my bag heavy

③ my heavy bag

④ heavy bag my

**4** Denis doesn't have _____ money.

① a      ② any

③ some      ④ many

[5-6] 빈칸에 들어갈 수 <u>없는</u> 것을 고르세요.

**5** He met a _____ singer.

① like

② popular

③ famous

④ handsome

**6** We need _____ tables.

① some

② many

③ much

④ a lot of

[7-8] 빈칸에 들어갈 말이 바르게 짝지어진 것을 고르세요.

**7**
- My father is _____.
- Are you _____ a letter now?

① laugh – write

② laugh – writing

③ laughing – write

④ laughing – writing

All our dreams can come true, if we have the courage to pursue them.

– Walt Disney

**8**

- There are _____ birds in the tree.
- Kate drank _____ water.

① any – many
② any – lots of
③ some – many
④ some – lots of

**9** 다음 문장을 부정문으로 바르게 바꾼 것을 고르세요.

They are dancing.

① They do not dancing.
② They not are dancing.
③ They are not dancing.
④ They are dancing not.

**10** 다음 문장을 우리말로 바르게 옮긴 것을 고르세요.

She is smiling brightly.

① 그녀는 밝게 웃었다.
② 그녀는 밝게 웃고 있다.
③ 그녀는 밝게 웃을 것이다.
④ 그녀는 밝게 웃고 있지 않다.

**11** 다음 우리말을 영어로 바르게 옮긴 것을 고르세요.

앨리스는 몇 개의 컵을 들고 있다.

① Alice is hold any cups.
② Alice is hold some cups.
③ Alice is holding any cups.
④ Alice is holding some cups.

**12** 다음 중 틀린 문장을 고르세요.

① The tiger is lying down.
② They are going to the zoo.
③ The man isn't wearing glasses.
④ Does your friend waiting outside?

**13** 다음 문장에서 틀린 부분을 찾아 바르게 고쳐 쓰세요.

Is she swiming in the sea?

_____ → _____

**14** 다음 우리말과 같은 뜻이 되도록 주어진 단어를 이용하여 문장을 완성하세요.

소피아는 신문을 읽고 있지 않다.

→ Sophia _____ the newspaper. (read)

# 나는 몇 점짜리 이성 친구일까?

으악! 어젯밤 지독한 악몽을 꾸었어요.
꿈에서 무시무시한 것에 쫓기고 있었는데, 그것은 무엇이었을까요?

A 코끼리 떼

B 소 떼

C 불을 뿜는 용

D 악마

결과는 p. 84에서 확인할 수 있습니다.

# UNIT 07 부사

## 다시 보기

지난 Unit에서 배운 내용을 다시 확인해 보세요.

### ☆ 형용사

James drives a **blue** car. 제임스는 파란 자동차를 운전한다.

The table is **round**. 그 테이블은 둥글다.

### ☆ 수와 양을 나타내는 형용사

I baked **some** cookies. 나는 쿠키를 몇 개 구웠다.

He doesn't have **any** friends. 그는 친구가 전혀 없다.

The bug has **many** legs. 그 벌레는 다리가 많다.

Camels don't drink **much** water. 낙타는 물을 많이 마시지 않는다.

**A lot of**[= **Lots of**] people laughed. 많은 사람들이 웃었다.

## 미리 보기

만화를 통해 이번 Unit에서 배울 내용을 미리 살펴보세요.

# 부사의 종류와 역할

A  Tom was at a baseball game.  톰은 야구 경기장에 있었다.

B  **Suddenly**, the ball flew toward him!  갑자기, 공이 그에게 날아왔다!

C  He **quickly** caught it.  그는 빠르게 그것을 잡았다.

D  It was a home run!  홈런이었다!

**예문 맛보기**

B, C의 Suddenly와 quickly로 문장의 내용이 더 흥미진진해졌어!

**1** **부사는 언제, 어디서, 어떻게, 얼마나** 등을 나타내는 말로, 우리말로는 '빠르게', '일찍' 같은 말들이 바로 부사입니다. 부사는 주로 '…**하게**'라고 해석하며, 문장의 의미를 더욱 풍부하게 만드는 역할을 합니다.

| 언제 | early 일찍 | today 오늘 | soon 곧 | now 지금, 이제 |
|---|---|---|---|---|
| 어디서 | up 위에 | down 아래에 | here 여기에 | there 저기에 |
| 어떻게 | well 잘 | slowly 느리게 | easily 쉽게 | kindly 친절하게 |
| 얼마나 | very 매우 | too 너무 | almost 거의 | really 아주 |

## Examples

He eats **slowly**. 그는 천천히 먹는다.

This hat is **too** big. 이 모자는 너무 크다.

Nicole sings **well**. 니콜은 노래를 잘 부른다.

**Sadly**, he left Korea. 슬프게도, 그는 한국을 떠났다.

**2** 부사는 주로 형용사를 규칙에 따라 바꾸어 만듭니다.

| 형용사의 형태 | 규칙 | Examples | |
|---|---|---|---|
| 대부분의 형용사 | 형용사+-ly | sad – sad**ly** | loud – loud**ly** |
| -le로 끝나는 형용사 | e를 빼고+-ly | simple – simp**ly** | gentle – gent**ly** |
| 「자음+y」로 끝나는 형용사 | y를 i로 고치고+-ly | lucky – luck**ily** | happy – happ**ily** |

**3** 형용사와 형태가 같은 부사도 있습니다.

early 이른 – **early** 일찍    high 높은 – **high** 높게    fast 빠른 – **fast** 빠르게

late 늦은 – **late** 늦게    low 낮은 – **low** 낮게    hard 열심인 – **hard** 열심히

## Examples

She left **early**. 그녀는 일찍 떠났다.

Airplanes fly **fast**. 비행기는 빠르게 난다.

# WARM UP

**A** 다음 중 부사를 고르고 그 뜻을 쓰세요.

school    soon    great    slowly

pretty    enjoy    too    catch    ugly

look    well    here    sad

1 부사: _____ 뜻: _____

2 부사: _____ 뜻: _____

3 부사: _____ 뜻: _____

4 부사: _____ 뜻: _____

5 부사: _____ 뜻: _____

**B** 다음 형용사를 부사로 바꿔 쓰세요.

1 sad → _____

2 careful → _____

3 loud → _____

4 easy → _____

5 fast → _____

6 happy → _____

7 simple → _____

**B**
careful 조심스러운
loud (소리가) 큰,
시끄러운
easy 쉬운
simple 단순한

# 빈도부사

**A** My brother **often** bothers me.  내 남동생은 나를 자주 귀찮게 한다.

**B** I am **sometimes** upset.  나는 가끔씩 화가 난다.

**C** But I **never** hate him.  그렇지만 나는 결코 그를 미워하지 않는다.

### 예문 맛보기

A~C의 often, sometimes, never를 빈도부사라고 해. 이 세 단어에는 어떤 차이가 있을까?

**1** **빈도부사**란 어떤 일이 **얼마나 자주 일어나는지**를 나타내는 부사입니다.

| | |
|---|---|
| 100% | always 항상 |
| | usually 보통, 대개 |
| | often 자주 |
| | sometimes 가끔 |
| 0% | never 결코 … 않다 |

### Examples

Ann **never** drinks coffee. 앤은 결코 커피를 마시지 않는다.

She **sometimes** walks to school. 그녀는 가끔 학교에 걸어간다.

He **often** buys bubble gum. 그는 자주 풍선껌을 산다.

We **usually** have lunch together. 우리는 보통 점심을 함께 먹는다.

Bell is **always** kind to others. 벨은 항상 다른 사람들에게 친절하다.

**2** 빈도부사는 **be동사의 뒤**나 **일반동사의 앞**에 위치합니다.

### Examples

[be동사 뒤]     She *is* **often** sick. 그녀는 자주 아프다.

            My parents *are* **usually** busy. 우리 부모님은 대개 바쁘시다.

[일반동사 앞]   I **always** *wear* glasses. 나는 항상 안경을 쓴다.

            He **sometimes** *cleans* his room. 그는 가끔 그의 방을 청소한다.

다음 문장에서 빈도부사에 ○ 하세요.

**1** He always has breakfast.

**2** I am usually free on weekends.

**3** They often stay at home in the evening.

# WARM UP

**A** 다음 빈도부사를 우리말과 바르게 연결하세요.

1 usually •          • a 항상

2 never •            • b 자주

3 sometimes •       • c 결코 … 않다

4 always •          • d 보통, 대개

5 often •           • e 가끔

**B** 다음 문장에서 often이 들어갈 위치에 ✓ 하세요.

1 Emma ① is ② sick.

2 I ① am ② hungry.

3 He ① cries ② loudly.

4 Paul ① looks ② tired.

5 They ① drink ② coffee.

6 Mary ① plays ② the ③ piano.

7 Betty ① is ② late ③ for school.

8 We ① have ② lunch ③ in the park.

**B**
loudly 큰 소리로
park 공원

**A** ( ) 안에서 알맞은 것을 고르세요.

1 He drives his car so ( fast / fastly ).

2 She ( safe / safely ) arrived in Africa.

3 ( Sad / Sadly ), my dog died last month.

4 She ( warm / warmly ) hugged her son.

5 Sam ( is always / always is ) honest.

6 The children ( are never / never are ) quiet.

7 We ( often watch / watch often ) cartoons on Sundays.

**B** 다음 빈칸에 알맞은 말을 〈보기〉에서 골라 쓰세요.

| 〈보기〉 | sometimes | always | usually | never | often |

100%

1 Lewis is _____ kind.

2 He _____ has sandwiches for lunch.

3 He _____ wears red shoes.

4 He _____ goes to concerts.

5 He is _____ late for work.

0%

**Vocabulary**

A
die 죽다
hug 포옹하다
son 아들
honest 정직한
quiet 조용한
cartoon 만화

B
concert 콘서트

**C** 다음 그림을 보고 빈칸에 알맞은 말을 〈보기〉에서 골라 쓰세요.

〈보기〉  quietly   slowly   brightly   wonderfully

1

Snails move _____.

2

People speak _____ in the library.

3

Mina sings _____.

4

The sun shines _____.

**D** 다음 우리말과 같은 뜻이 되도록 주어진 단어를 알맞은 형태로 쓰세요.

D
laugh (소리내어) 웃다
stop 멈추다, 서다
brush one's hair
머리를 빗다
wake up
깨다, 일어나다

1 윌리엄은 행복하게 웃었다. (happy)

→ William laughed _____.

2 그 버스는 갑자기 멈췄다. (sudden)

→ The bus _____ stopped.

3 루시는 그녀의 머리를 부드럽게 빗었다. (gentle)

→ Lucy _____ brushed her hair.

4 너희 할머니는 일찍 일어나시니? (early)

→ Does your grandmother wake up _____?

**E** 다음 표를 보고 빈칸에 알맞은 말을 쓰세요.

| List | always | usually | often | sometimes | never |
|------|--------|---------|-------|-----------|-------|
| **Self-Check Chart** | | | | | Name: *Andy* |
| 1 sleep late at night | ☐ | ☑ | ☐ | ☐ | ☐ |
| 2 eat fast food | ☐ | ☐ | ☐ | ☐ | ☑ |
| 3 skip breakfast | ☑ | ☐ | ☐ | ☐ | ☐ |
| 4 be sick | ☐ | ☐ | ☐ | ☑ | ☐ |
| 5 be tired | ☐ | ☐ | ☑ | ☐ | ☐ |

1 Andy _____ _____ late at night.

2 He _____ _____ fast food.

3 He _____ _____ breakfast.

4 He _____ _____ _____ .

5 He _____ _____ _____ .

**F** 다음 문장에서 밑줄 친 부분을 바르게 고쳐 쓰세요.

1 The old man walks <u>strange</u>.　→　_____

2 She <u>carefuly</u> lifted the box.　→　_____

3 The stars shine <u>beautifuily</u>.　→　_____

4 The subway <u>usually is</u> crowded. →　_____

5 I <u>cry sometimes</u> in my room.　→　_____

6 He solved the problem <u>easy</u>.　→　_____

**F**
strange 이상한
lift 들어 올리다
subway 지하철
crowded 혼잡한
solve 해결하다
problem 문제

**A** 다음 ( ) 안에서 알맞은 것을 고르고, 문장을 우리말로 해석하세요.

1 The cat jumped ( high / highly ).

→ _____

2 The boys danced ( good / well ).

→ _____

3 I play the song ( perfect / perfectly ).

→ _____

4 ( Lucky / Luckily ), she won the gold medal.

→ _____

**B** 다음 우리말과 같은 뜻이 되도록 ( ) 안의 말을 바르게 배열하세요.

1 그는 절대 공포 영화를 보지 않는다.
(never / he / watches / scary movies)

→ _____

2 그녀는 항상 좋은 친구이다.
(is / always / she / a good friend)

→ _____

3 짐은 가끔 박물관을 방문한다.
(Jim / visits / sometimes / museums)

→ _____

4 나의 부모님은 자주 가난한 사람들을 돕는다.
(help / often / poor people / my parents)

→ _____

**A**
jump 뛰다, 점프하다
perfect 완벽한
win 이기다; *따다
gold medal 금메달

**B**
scary 무서운
museum 박물관
poor 가난한
people 사람들
parents 부모님

부사 ▪ **83**

# 나는 몇 점짜리 이성 친구일까?

**A** **코끼리 떼** 를 선택한 당신은
**50** 점 짜리 이성 친구!
당신은 이성 친구가 잘해줘도
고마운 마음을 표현할 줄 모르는군요.
다음에 이성 친구가 선물을 주면
꼭 고맙다고 말해보세요.

자, 선물!!

고... 고마워!

후비적~

**B** **소 떼** 를 선택한 당신은
**25** 점 짜리 이성 친구!
당신은 매우 현실적인 사람이라,
로맨틱한 분위기를 만들 줄 모르네요.
가끔씩은 이성 친구에게
영화 속 주인공처럼 로맨틱한 말을 해보세요.

**C** **불을 뿜는 용** 을 선택한 당신은
**100** 점 짜리 이성 친구!
당신은 이성 친구가 원하는
바를 항상 잘 들어주고,
그 사람을 위해서는 뭐든지 해줄 수 있는
100점짜리 이성 친구네요.

**D** **악마** 를 선택한 당신은
**75** 점 짜리 이성 친구!
당신은 만족을 잘 하고
이성친구에게 잔소리를
잘 하지 않아요. 그래서 이성친구는
당신을 꽤 괜찮은 사람이라고 생각하고 있어요.

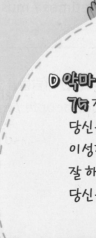

# 전치사

## 다시 보기

지난 Unit에서 배운 내용을 다시 확인해 보세요.

### ☆ 부사

He eats **slowly**. 그는 천천히 먹는다.
This hat is **too** big. 이 모자는 너무 크다.

### ☆ 빈도부사

Ann **never** drinks coffee. 앤은 결코 커피를 마시지 않는다.
She **sometimes** walks to school. 그녀는 가끔 학교에 걸어간다.
He **often** buys bubble gum. 그는 자주 풍선껌을 산다.
We **usually** have lunch together. 우리는 보통 점심을 함께 먹는다.
Bell is **always** kind to others. 벨은 항상 다른 사람들에게 친절하다.

## 미리 보기

만화를 통해 이번 Unit에서 배울 내용을 미리 살펴보세요.

# 위치를 나타내는 전치사

**A** Ella is a witch.  엘라는 마녀이다.

**B** She lives **in** an old house.  그녀는 오래된 집에 산다.

**C** The moon is **over** the house.  집 위에 달이 떠 있다.

**예문맛보기**

B의 in, C의 over와 같은 단어를 전치사라고 해.

**1** **전치사**는 명사나 대명사 앞에 쓰여서 **위치, 시간** 등을 나타내 주는 말입니다. 우리말로는 '… 위에', '… 후에'와 같은 말들이 바로 전치사입니다.

**2** 다음은 **위치**를 나타내는 대표적인 전치사입니다.

| in … 안에 | under … 아래에 | on … 위에 (표면에 닿은) |
|---|---|---|
| A mouse is **in** the box.<br>쥐 한 마리가 상자 안에 있다. | A bag is **under** the chair.<br>가방이 의자 아래에 있다. | A doll is **on** the bed.<br>인형이 침대 위에 있다. |

| at … 에(서) | behind … 뒤에 | in front of … 앞에 |
|---|---|---|
| They are **at** the cafe.<br>그들은 카페에 있다. | Tina is **behind** the tree.<br>티나는 나무 뒤에 있다. | I am **in front of** the car.<br>나는 차 앞에 있다. |

| over<br>… 위에 (표면과 떨어진),<br>… 너머에 | next to … 옆에 | between … 사이에 |
|---|---|---|
| A picture is **over** the bed.<br>그림이 침대 위에 있다. | A ball is **next to** the box.<br>공이 상자 옆에 있다. | He is **between** the lion and the tiger.<br>그는 사자와 호랑이 사이에 있다. |

# WARM UP

**A** 다음 전치사의 뜻을 쓰세요.

1  at _____

2  on _____

3  in _____

4  behind _____

5  under _____

6  over _____

7  next to _____

8  in front of _____

9  between _____

**B** 다음 문장에서 주어진 전치사가 들어갈 위치에 ✓ 하세요.

1　　on　　　　My cat ① is ② lying ③ me.

2　　in　　　　A bug ① is ② the ③ soup.

3　　next to　　A pencil ① is ② the book.

4　　behind　　A doll ① is ② the bag ③.

5　　over　　　There ① is ② a bridge ③ the river.

**B**
lie 누워 있다, 눕다
bridge 다리
river 강

전치사 ■ **87**

# 시간을 나타내는 전치사

**A** We went to a restaurant.  우리는 한 식당에 갔다.

**B** There were many people.  사람들이 많았다.

**C** We waited **for** an hour.  우리는 한 시간 동안 기다렸다.

C의 for처럼, 시간을 나타내는 다양한 전치사에 대해 알아보자!

**1** 전치사 **at, on, in**은 위치뿐만 아니라, **시간**을 나타내기도 합니다. 모두 '···에'라고 해석되지만, 그 쓰임이 각각 다릅니다.

| 전치사 | 쓰임 | Examples | |
|---|---|---|---|
| at | 시각, 특정한 때 | **at** 8:30 a.m. 오전 8시 30분에 | **at** night 밤에 |
| on | 날짜, 요일, 특정한 날 | **on** June 21 6월 21일에<br>**on** my birthday 내 생일에 | **on** Friday 금요일에<br>**on** the weekend 주말에 |
| in | 오전, 오후, 월, 계절, 연도 | **in** the morning 아침에<br>**in** summer 여름에 | **in** March 3월에<br>**in** 2015 2015년에 |

**2** **시간**을 나타내는 전치사에는 **before, after, for** 등도 있습니다.

| 전치사 | 의미 | Examples | |
|---|---|---|---|
| before | ··· 전에 | **before** eight o'clock 8시 전에 | **before** sunset 일몰 전에 |
| after | ··· 후에 | **after** eight o'clock 8시 후에 | **after** school 방과 후에 |
| for | ··· 동안 | **for** five years 5년 동안 | **for** an hour 한 시간 동안 |

전치사는 시간과 위치 이외에도 다양한 의미를 나타냅니다.

**of** ···의    **with** ···와 함께    **for** ···을 위해    **about** ···에 관해    **to** ···으로, ···에게

**a piece of** the cake 케이크의 한 조각    **with** a cat 고양이와 함께    **for** my mother 어머니를 위해
**about** the movie 그 영화에 관해    **to** school 학교로 / **to** Daniel 다니엘에게

# WARM UP

**A** 다음 우리말과 같은 뜻이 되도록 ( ) 안에서 알맞은 것을 고르세요.

1 너를 위해          ( with / for ) you

2 병원으로          ( for / to ) the hospital

3 우주에 관해          ( of / about ) the universe

4 3일 동안          ( for / on ) three days

5 나의 어머니께          ( to / with ) my mother

6 저녁 식사 후에          ( before / after ) dinner

7 친구들과 함께          ( with / about ) friends

8 언덕의 꼭대기          the top ( of / to ) the hill

**A**
hospital 병원
universe 우주
top 꼭대기, 정상
hill 언덕, 산

**B** 빈칸에 알맞은 전치사를 〈보기〉에서 골라 쓰세요.

〈보기〉    at      on      in

1 _____ 2012      6 _____ two o'clock

2 _____ night      7 _____ my birthday

3 _____ April      8 _____ the afternoon

4 _____ 7:20 a.m.      9 _____ Christmas

5 _____ Tuesday      10 _____ spring

**B**
noon 정오, 낮 12시
April 4월
Tuesday 화요일
afternoon 오후
spring 봄

**A** ( ) 안에서 알맞은 것을 고르세요.

1 Paul sat ( on / over ) the chair.

2 She studied ( at / for ) an hour.

3 My mother wakes up ( at / in ) six o'clock.

4 We waited for you ( in / on ) front of the bakery.

5 They watched movies together ( for / after ) dinner.

**B** 다음 그림을 보고 빈칸에 알맞은 전치사를 〈보기〉에서 골라 쓰세요.

B
leaf (나뭇)잎
path 길
rainbow 무지개
sea 바다
put 놓다, 두다
vase 꽃병
teddy bear 곰 인형

〈보기〉 behind    on    between    over

1

Some leaves are _____ the path.

2

There is a rainbow _____ the sea.

3

I put the vase _____ the teddy bear.

4

The red car is _____ the black car and the truck.

**C** 다음 그림을 보고 빈칸에 at, on, in 중 알맞은 것을 쓰세요.

**1**

The concert is _____ December.

It starts _____ 9 p.m.

**2**

The party is _____ Halloween.

It starts _____ the evening.

**3**

The festival begins _____ July 2.

The first festival was _____ 1990.

ⓒ
December 12월
start 시작하다
since …부터[이후]
festival 축제
begin 시작하다
first 첫, 첫 번째의

**D** 우리말과 같은 뜻이 되도록 주어진 말과 적절한 전치사를 사용하여 문장을 완성하세요.

1 그 고양이는 테이블 밑에 있다. (the table)

→ The cat is _____.

2 그녀는 여섯 시 전에 집에 간다. (six o'clock)

→ She goes home _____.

3 그들은 스페인에 7일 동안 머물렀다. (seven days)

→ They stayed in Spain _____.

4 우리는 지하철역에서 만났다. (the subway station)

→ We met _____.

ⓓ
stay 머무르다
subway station
지하철역

**E** 다음 그림을 보고 빈칸에 알맞은 전치사를 쓰세요.

1 A doghouse is _____ the house.

2 A dog is _____ the doghouse.

3 A bicycle is _____ the doghouse.

4 A tree is _____ the bicycle.

**F** 다음 빈칸에 알맞은 전치사를 〈보기〉에서 골라 쓰세요.

〈보기〉 at in with to

Today was our school picnic!

1 I got up very early _____ the morning.

2 We went _____ the Great Temple.

3 We arrived there _____ 1 p.m.

4 I had lunch _____ my classmates.

 다음 문장을 우리말로 해석하세요.

**1** The ball flew over the fence.

→ _____

**2** I don't know the name of the flower.

→ _____

**3** We took a walk for thirty minutes.

→ _____

**4** The restaurant is between the bank and the hospital.

→ _____

**B** 다음 문장에서 <u>틀린</u> 부분을 고쳐 문장을 다시 쓰세요.

B
May 5월
often 자주
have a party
파티를 열다
go jogging
조깅하러 가다

**1** Linda is next her sister.

→ _____

**2** Roses are beautiful on May.

→ _____

**3** I often eat ice cream at summer.

→ _____

**4** Walter had a party in his birthday.

→ _____

**5** I go jogging with my sister on the afternoon.

→ _____

**1** 다음 중 틀린 것을 고르세요.

① at night

② at winter

③ for two days

④ on Tuesday

**2** 부사와 그 뜻이 잘못 연결된 것을 고르세요.

① always – 항상

② often – 자주, 종종

③ never – 보통, 대개

④ sometimes – 가끔

[3-4] 빈칸에 들어갈 말로 알맞은 것을 고르세요.

**3**    My brother swims _____.

① well

② good

③ enjoy

④ careful

**4**    I travelled to Africa _____ 2013.

① to

② on

③ at

④ in

[5-6] 빈칸에 들어갈 수 없는 것을 고르세요.

**5**    She came home _____.

① late

② early

③ safely

④ walk

**6**    We threw a party on _____.

① seven o'clock

② Christmas Day

③ Thursday

④ my birthday

**7** 빈칸에 들어갈 말이 바르게 짝지어진 것을 고르세요.

• He went _____ the hospital.

• They are talking _____ the computer game.

① to – for

② with – to

③ to – about

④ with – about

[8-9] 다음 중 <u>틀린</u> 문장을 고르세요.

**8**
① Jane always is polite.
② He is sometimes sad.
③ I often meet my cousins.
④ She never eats lemons.

**9**
① Apple juice is at the bottle.
② I felt tired in the morning.
③ The bowls are on the table.
④ Susan went hiking with her father.

**10** 다음 중 올바른 문장을 고르세요.
① He helped me kind.
② She speaks Chinese well.
③ Tina called me very loud.
④ Mike careful listen to the music.

**11** 빈칸에 공통으로 들어갈 말을 쓰세요.

• I met Tiffany _____ the theater.
• The show starts _____ 7:30 p.m.

[12-13] 다음 우리말과 같은 뜻이 되도록 빈칸에 알맞은 말을 쓰세요.

**12**
그는 책상 앞에 서 있다.

→ He is standing _____ the desk.

**13**
집 옆에 나무가 있다.

→ There is a tree _____ the house.

**14** 다음 문장을 우리말로 해석하세요.

Lisa always reads books too slowly.

→ _____

**15** <u>틀린</u> 부분을 찾아 바르게 고쳐 쓰세요.

The runner ran so fastly.

_____ → _____

# 재미있는 영어 표현

영어에는 "have two left feet"이라는 표현이 있어요.
아래 그림을 보고 무슨 뜻일지 생각해 보세요.

have two left feet 몸치이다, 춤을 잘 못 추다
"have two left feet"을 단어 그대로 해석하면 '왼발을 두 개 갖고 있다'라는 뜻이죠?
왼발만 두 개라면 춤을 잘 출 수 없기 때문에 '몸치'를 가리킬 때 이 표현을 써요.

## Example

A: Look! Jake is dancing. 봐! 제이크가 춤을 추고 있어.
B: He has two left feet! 그는 몸치구나!
A: It's so funny! 정말 웃기다!

# UNIT 09  숫자 표현

## 다시 보기

지난 Unit에서 배운 내용을 다시 확인해 보세요.

### ☆ 위치를 나타내는 전치사

A mouse is **in** the box. 쥐 한 마리가 상자 안에 있다.
A bag is **under** the chair. 가방이 의자 아래에 있다.
A doll is **on** the bed. 인형이 침대 위에 있다.
They are **at** the cafe. 그들은 카페에 있다.
Tina is **behind** the tree. 티나는 나무 뒤에 있다.
I am **in front of** the car. 나는 차 앞에 있다.

### ☆ 시간을 나타내는 전치사

**at** night 밤에                **on** Friday 금요일에           **in** the morning 아침에

**before** eight o'clock 8시 전에   **after** school 방과 후에       **for** an hour 한 시간 동안

## 미리 보기

만화를 통해 이번 Unit에서 배울 내용을 미리 살펴보세요.

# 기수와 서수

A  There are **three** balls.  세 개의 공이 있다.

B  The **first** one is a baseball.  첫 번째 공은 야구공이다.

C  The **second** one is a soccer ball.  두 번째 공은 축구공이다.

D  The **third** one is a basketball.  세 번째 공은 농구공이다.

**예문 맛보기**

개수를 나타내는 표현과 순서를 나타내는 표현은 무엇이 다를까?

**1**  **기수**는 '한 개', '두 개'처럼 **개수**를 셀 때 쓰는 말입니다. **서수**는 '첫 번째', '두 번째'처럼 **순서**를 나타내는 말입니다.

**2**  기수와 서수는 다음과 같은 형태로 씁니다.

| 숫자 | 기수 | 서수 | 숫자 | 기수 | 서수 | 숫자 | 기수 | 서수 |
|------|------|------|------|------|------|------|------|------|
| 1 | one | first | 11 | eleven | eleventh | 30 | thirty | thirtieth |
| 2 | two | second | 12 | twelve | twelfth | 40 | forty | fortieth |
| 3 | three | third | 13 | thirteen | thirteenth | 50 | fifty | fiftieth |
| 4 | four | fourth | 14 | fourteen | fourteenth | 75 | seventy-five | seventy-fifth |
| 5 | five | fifth | 15 | fifteen | fifteenth | 90 | ninety | ninetieth |
| 6 | six | sixth | 16 | sixteen | sixteenth | 100 | one hundred | one hundredth |
| 7 | seven | seventh | 17 | seventeen | seventeenth | 200 | two hundred | two hundredth |
| 8 | eight | eighth | 18 | eighteen | eighteenth | | | |
| 9 | nine | ninth | 19 | nineteen | nineteenth | | | |
| 10 | ten | tenth | 20 | twenty | twentieth | | | |

**Examples**

He arrived at **one** o'clock. 그는 한 시에 도착했다.

Monday is the **first** day of the week. 월요일은 한 주의 첫 번째 날이다.

I have **five** dogs. 나는 개 다섯 마리가 있다.

This is the **fifth** floor. 이곳은 5층(다섯 번째 층)이다.

There are **twelve** doughnuts in the box. 상자 안에 열두 개의 도넛이 있다.

December is the **twelfth** month of the year. 12월은 한 해의 열두 번째 달이다.

# WARM UP

**Vocabulary**

A
build (건물을) 짓다
enough 충분한
daughter 딸
textbook 교과서
understand
이해하다
congratulate
축하하다

**A** 다음 서수가 나타내는 순서를 오른쪽 단어에서 찾아 ○ 하세요.

1   first   ⓑ u i l d

2   second   e n o u g h

3   sixth   d a u g h t e r

4   third   a f t e r n o o n

5   fifth   t e x t b o o k

6   eighth   u n d e r s t a n d

7   twelfth   c o n g r a t u l a t e

**B** 다음 우리말과 같은 뜻이 되도록 (   ) 안에서 알맞은 것을 고르세요.

B
grade 학년
floor 층

1   첫사랑   ( first / one ) love

2   자동차 세 대   ( three / third ) cars

3   4학년   the ( four / fourth ) grade

4   2층   the ( two / second ) floor

5   학교 첫 날   the ( first / one ) day of school

6   학생 백 명   ( one hundredth / one hundred ) students

# 연도, 날짜, 나이

**A** Today is **December 31, 2016.**  오늘은 2016년 12월 31일이다.

**B** I am **eleven years old.**  나는 열한 살이다.

**C** The clock hits midnight.  시계가 자정을 가리킨다.

**D** Now, I am **a twelve-year-old boy!**  이제, 나는 열두 살 소년이다!

### 예문 맛보기

영어로 날짜와 나이를 어떻게 표현하는지 살펴봐.

**1**  **연도:** 영어에서 연도는 보통 **두 자리씩 끊어 읽습니다.** 단, 2000년 이후는 주로 끊어 읽지 않고, 일반 숫자처럼 읽습니다.

### Examples

| | |
|---|---|
| 1896년  eighteen˅ninety-six | 2008년  two thousand eight |
| 1907년  nineteen˅oh seven | 2017년  two thousand seventeen |
| 1999년  nineteen˅ninety-nine | 2020년  two thousand twenty |

**2**  **날짜:** 우리말로 날짜는 '2015년 10월 11일 일요일'처럼 「연도–월–일–요일」 순으로 쓰죠? 하지만 영어에서는 우리말과 달리 「**요일–월–일–연도**」의 순서로 씁니다.

<u>Sunday,</u> <u>October</u> <u>11,</u> <u>2015</u>  2015년 10월 11일 일요일
　요일　　　월　　　일　　연도

> **BUDDY'S TIPS**
> 날짜를 읽을 때는 서수로 읽어야 해.
> April 9 (April ninth) 4월 9일
> June 30 (June thirtieth) 6월 30일

### Examples

**Tuesday, November 4, 1788**  1788년 11월 4일 화요일

**Friday, September 28, 2005**  2005년 9월 28일 금요일

**Monday, May 13, 2013**  2013년 5월 13일 월요일

**Sunday, December 17, 1984**  1984년 12월 17일 일요일

*영어의 요일과 월 표현은 p.106에서 더 볼 수 있습니다.

**3**  **나이:** 나이는 「**숫자+years old**」 또는 「**a/an+숫자-year-old+명사**」의 형태로 표현할 수 있습니다.

### Examples

I am **thirteen years old.** 나는 열세 살이다.

I am **a thirteen-year-old girl.** 나는 열세 살 소녀이다.

Jessica is **twenty years old.** 제시카는 스무 살이다.

Jessica is **a twenty-year-old student.** 제시카는 스무 살 학생이다.

Daniel is **eleven years old.** 다니엘은 열한 살이다.

Daniel is **an eleven-year-old boy.** 다니엘은 열한 살 소년이다.

# WARM UP

## A 알맞은 연도를 찾아 바르게 연결하세요.

1 two thousand eleven •          • a 1865

2 two thousand eight •          • b 2008

3 nineteen eighty-four •          • c 2017

4 eighteen sixty-five •          • d 1984

5 two thousand seventeen •          • e 2011

6 nineteen oh seven •          • f 1907

## B 다음 우리말과 일치하는 표현을 고르세요.

1 2020년
   a two thousand twenty
   b two thousand twentieth

2 2015년 10월 11일 금요일
   a 2015, October 11, Friday
   b Friday, October 11, 2015

3 척은 열두 살이다.
   a Chuck is twelve years old.
   b Chuck is twelve-years-old.

4 1995년
   a nineteen ninety-five
   b one thousand nine hundred ninety-five

B
October 10월
Friday 금요일

 ( ) 안에서 알맞은 것을 고르세요.

1 He is ( fifteen-year-old / fifteen years old ).

2 The ( one / first ) show starts at 7 p.m.

3 The train leaves at ( five / fifth ) o'clock.

4 The snack bar is on the ( ninth / nine ) floor.

5 Today is ( Monday, July 11 / July 11, Monday ).

6 I'm the ( two / second ) son in my family.

7 My uncle is ( thirty years old / thirty-years-old man ).

8 I'm a ( seventeen-year-old / seventeen years old ) girl.

**A**

leave
떠나다, 출발하다
snack bar
스낵바, 간이식당
Monday 월요일
July 7월
son 아들
uncle 삼촌

**B** 다음 연도를 영어로 소리나는 대로 쓰세요.

| | | |
|---|---|---|
| 1 | 1988년 | nineteen eighty-eight |
| 2 | 2016년 | |
| 3 | 1845년 | |
| 4 | 2006년 | |
| 5 | 1993년 | |
| 6 | 2005년 | |

C 다음 그림을 보고 빈칸에 알맞은 말을 쓰세요.

This is Katie's bookshelf.

1 Cute dolls are on the
___first___ shelf.

2 There are many books on
the _____ shelf.

3 An alarm clock is on the
_____ shelf.

4 There are plants on the
_____ shelf.

D 다음 그림의 날짜를 영어로 쓰세요.

1

Thursday, November 4, 1970

2

_____

3

_____

4

_____

**E** 다음 우리말과 같은 뜻이 되도록 빈칸에 알맞은 말을 쓰세요.

1 4월 1일은 만우절이다.

→ _____ is April Fool's Day.

2 상자에 계란 열두 개가 있다.

→ There are _____ eggs in the box.

3 그 세일은 이틀 전에 시작했다.

→ The sale started _____ days ago.

4 오늘은 할아버지의 일흔 번째 생신이다.

→ Today is my grandfather's _____ birthday.

**F** 다음 표를 보고 빈칸에 알맞은 말을 쓰세요.

| 이름 | 나이 | 생년월일 |
|------|------|---------|
| Henry | 11 | 2005년 8월 27일 |
| Hanna | 12 | 2004년 4월 8일 |
| Luke | 13 | 2003년 12월 13일 |

1 Henry is _____ old.

2 He was born on _____ .

3 Hanna is a _____ girl.

4 She was born on _____ .

5 Luke is _____ old.

6 He was born on _____ .

 **A** 밑줄 친 부분에 유의하여 다음 문장을 우리말로 해석하세요.

**1** There are <u>three</u> monkeys in the cage.

→ _____

**2** I live on the <u>twelfth</u> floor.

→ _____

**3** Olivia is in <u>sixth</u> grade.

→ _____

**4** The key is in the <u>first</u> drawer.

→ _____

**B** 다음 문장에서 <u>틀린</u> 부분을 고쳐 문장을 다시 쓰세요.

**1** Tyler met Kate tenth years ago.

→ _____

**2** My little sister is sixth-year-old.

→ _____

**3** The fiveth color of the rainbow is blue.

→ _____

**4** He entered the school on 1996, March 1.

→ _____

**5** Thanksgiving Day is on the four Thursday of November.

→ _____

**Vocabulary**

**A**
cage 우리
drawer 서랍

**B**
rainbow 무지개
enter
들어가다; *입학하다
March 3월
Thanksgiving Day
추수감사절

숫자 표현 ■ **105**

# 요일과 월 표현

## ★ 요일 (Days of the Week)

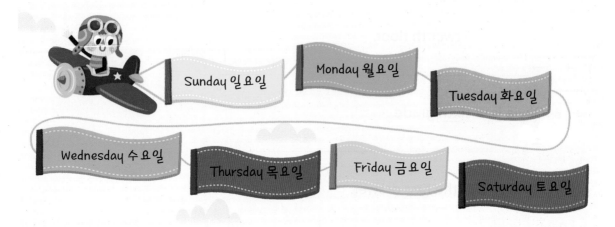

Sunday 일요일

Monday 월요일

Tuesday 화요일

Wednesday 수요일

Thursday 목요일

Friday 금요일

Saturday 토요일

## ★ 월 (Months of the Year)

January - 1월

February - 2월

March - 3월

April - 4월

May - 5월

June - 6월

July - 7월

August - 8월

September - 9월

October - 10월

November - 11월

December - 12월

# 비인칭 주어 it

## 다시 보기

지난 Unit에서 배운 내용을 다시 확인해 보세요.

### ☆ 기수와 서수

He arrived at **one** o'clock. 그는 한 시에 도착했다.
Monday is the **first** day of the week. 월요일은 한 주의 첫 번째 날이다.
I have **five** dogs. 나는 개 다섯 마리가 있다.
This is the **fifth** floor. 이곳은 5층(다섯 번째 층)이다.

### ☆ 연도, 날짜, 나이

- 연도　 nineteen ninety-nine 1999년
　　　　 two thousand eight 2008년
- 날짜　 Friday, September 28, 2005 2005년 9월 28일 금요일
- 나이　 I am thirteen years old. 나는 열세 살이다.
　　　　 I am a thirteen-year-old girl. 나는 열세 살 소녀이다.

## 미리 보기

만화를 통해 이번 Unit에서 배울 내용을 미리 살펴보세요.

# 비인칭 주어 it

**A** **It** is my birthday. 내 생일이다.

**B** This is the dress for my party. 이것은 내 파티를 위한 드레스이다.

**C** **It** is lovely. 그것은 아주 멋지다.

**예문 맛보기**

A와 C의 It은 모양은 같지만 쓰임이 달라!

**1** it은 '그것'이라는 뜻의 대명사로 쓰이기도 하지만, **날짜, 날씨, 거리** 등을 나타낼 때도 쓰입니다. 이때 사용되는 it을 **비인칭 주어**라고 합니다. 비인칭 주어는 특별한 뜻은 없으므로 우리말로 따로 해석하지 않습니다.

**2** 비인칭 주어 it은 **날짜**와 **요일**을 나타낼 때 씁니다.

**Examples**

A: What's the date today? 오늘이 며칠이니?　　　　B: **It is March 24.** 3월 24일이야.

A: What day is **it** today? 오늘이 무슨 요일이니?　　B: **It's Tuesday.** 화요일이야.

**3** 비인칭 주어 it은 **거리**를 나타낼 때 씁니다.

**Examples**

**It** is far. (거리가) 멀다.

**It's** not far from here. 여기서 멀지 않다.

A: How far is **it**? 얼마나 머니?　　　　　　　　B: **It is three kilometers.** 3킬로미터 거리야.

**4** 비인칭 주어 it은 **날씨**와 **계절**을 나타낼 때 씁니다.

**Examples**

A: How is the weather? 날씨가 어떠니?　　　　　　B: **It is sunny.** 화창해.

A: What season is **it**? 무슨 계절이니?　　　　　　B: **It's summer.** 여름이야.

**PLUS 날씨를 나타내는 표현**

| | | | | |
|---|---|---|---|---|
| fine 맑은 | sunny 화창한 | warm 따뜻한 | hot 더운 | cool 시원한 |
| cold 추운 | windy 바람 부는 | cloudy 구름 낀 | rainy 비 오는 | snowy 눈 오는 |

# WARM UP

**A** 밑줄 친 It이 나타내는 것을 바르게 연결하세요.

1 <u>It</u> is a fine day.  •

2 <u>It</u> is November 28. •

3 <u>It</u> is close to here. •

4 <u>It</u>'s Monday.  •

5 <u>It</u>'s winter.  •

• **a** 거리

• **b** 날씨

• **c** 요일

• **d** 날짜

• **e** 계절

**B** 밑줄 친 It이 비인칭 주어로 쓰인 문장에 ✓ 하세요.

1 <u>It</u> is very far. ☐

2 <u>It</u> is hot water. ☐

3 <u>It</u> is a big lion. ☐

4 <u>It</u> is a rainy day. ☐

5 <u>It</u>'s cold outside. ☐

6 <u>It</u>'s not summer. ☐

7 <u>It</u> is Tuesday. ☐

8 <u>It</u>'s a Christmas gift. ☐

# 시간 표현

A  **It** is seven fifty now.  지금은 7시 50분이다.

B  I'm running to school.  나는 학교로 뛰어가고 있다.

C  The test starts at eight **o'clock**.  시험이 8시에 시작한다.

D  I only have ten minutes.  10분밖에 안 남았다.

### 예문 맛보기

영어로 시간은 어떻게 표현하는지 알아보자!

**1**  **비인칭 주어 it**은 **시간**을 나타낼 때도 씁니다.

**2**  영어에서 시간은 보통 시와 분을 순서대로 읽어 표현합니다. **정각**일 때는 **o'clock**을 써서 표현하기도 합니다.

### Examples

It's six fifteen. 6시 15분이다.　　　　**It** is nine twenty. 9시 20분이다.

A: What time is **it**? 몇 시니?　　　　B: **It's** two. / **It's** two **o'clock**. 2시야.

**3**  시간을 나타낼 때 함께 쓰이는 표현으로 **past**와 **to**가 있습니다. '… past ~'는 '~시 …분', '… to ~'는 '~시 …분 전'이라고 해석합니다.

### Examples

It's ten **past** three. 3시 10분이다. (= It's three ten.)

It's five **to** eight. 8시 5분 전이다. (= It's seven fifty-five. 7시 55분이다.)

**4**  30분은 **half**를 써서 나타내기도 합니다.

### Examples

It's **half** past three. 3시 30분이다. (= It's three thirty.)

It is **half** past seven. 7시 30분이다. (= It is seven thirty.)

> **BUDDY'S TIPS**
> past는 '…을 지나',
> to는 '…로, …을 향해'라는 뜻이야.

It's two.
It's two o'clock.

It's four thirty.
It's half past four.

It's six fifty.
It's ten to seven.

It's five twenty.
It's twenty past five.

# WARM UP

 다음 그림과 일치하는 문장을 고르세요.

**1**

a It is three ten.

b It is three o'clock.

**2**

a It's seven twenty.

b It's twenty seven.

**3**

a It's half past one.

b It's one thirteen.

**4**

a It is nine past ten.

b It's ten past nine.

 다음 문장을 우리말과 바르게 연결하세요.

1 It's five ten.    •

2 It's five thirty.    •

3 It's five to ten.    •

4 It's ten to five.    •

5 It's five o'clock.    •

•  a 5시 정각이다.

•  b 5시 10분 전이다.

•  c 5시 10분이다.

•  d 5시 30분이다.

•  e 10시 5분 전이다.

**A** ( ) 안에서 알맞은 것을 고르세요.

1 ( It / There ) is far.

2 ( Now / It ) is a hot day.

3 ( It / Here ) is Wednesday.

4 ( It / This ) is five thirty.

5 ( It / There ) is summer in Japan.

6 ( That / It ) is September 30 today.

**B** 다음 그림을 보고 〈보기〉의 단어를 이용하여 문장을 완성하세요.

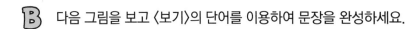

〈보기〉 cloudy   sunny   snowy   windy

1

_____ is _____ today.

2

_____ is _____ today.

3

_____ is _____ today.

4

_____ is a _____ day today.

C 다음 그림을 보고 빈칸에 past와 to 중 알맞은 것을 쓰세요.

1

It is five _____ nine.

2

It is twenty _____ one.

3

It is ten _____ two.

4

It is half _____ twelve.

D 우리말과 같은 뜻이 되도록 주어진 말을 이용하여 문장을 완성하세요.

D
spring 봄
from …에서, …부터

1 목요일이다. (Thursday)

→ _____ is _____ .

2 지금은 봄이다. (spring)

→ _____ is _____ now.

3 일곱 시 정각이 아니다. (o'clock)

→ _____ is not _____ _____ .

4 여기에서 2킬로미터 거리이다. (two kilometers)

→ _____ is _____ _____ from here.

**E** 두 문장이 같은 뜻이 되도록 빈칸에 알맞은 말을 쓰세요.

**1** It's four. → It's _____ _____.

**2** It is one fifty-five. → It is _____ to two.

**3** It is half past nine. → It is _____ thirty.

**4** It is ten twenty. → It is _____ past _____.

**5** It is two fifty. → It is _____ to _____.

**6** It is twenty to seven. → It is _____ _____.

**F** 다음 그림을 보고 빈칸에 알맞은 말을 쓰세요.

**F**
May 5월
Monday 월요일
weather 날씨
time 시간
month 달, 월

**1** A: How is the weather?     B: _____ sunny.

**2** A: What time is it now?     B: _____ to four.

**3** A: What month is it?     B: _____

**4** A: What day is it?     B: _____

 **A** 다음 문장에서 <u>틀린</u> 부분을 고쳐 문장을 다시 쓰세요.

**1** Now is Tuesday.

→ _____

**2** That is winter in Korea.

→ _____

**3** This is August 28 today.

→ _____

**4** There is five kilometers from here.

→ _____

**B** 주어진 말을 이용하여 우리말에 맞게 영작하세요.

**1** 어린이날이다. (Children's Day)

→ _____

**2** 11시 정각이다. (o'clock)

→ _____

**3** 8시 10분이다. (past)

→ _____

**4** 비 오는 날이다. (a rainy day)

→ _____

**5** 우리 집에서 멀지 않다. (far from my house)

→ _____

**Vocabulary**

**A**
winter 겨울
August 8월

**B**
Children's Day
어린이날

**1** 다음 중 연도를 읽는 방법이 <u>틀린</u> 것을 고르세요.

① 1419년 – fourteen nineteen

② 1986년 – nineteen eighty-six

③ 2004년 – two thousand four

④ 1690년 – one hundred sixty ninety

**2** 밑줄 친 It의 쓰임이 <u>다른</u> 하나를 고르세요.

① <u>It</u> is Thursday.

② <u>It</u> is my jacket.

③ <u>It</u> is a sunny day.

④ <u>It</u> is five o'clock.

**3** 기수와 서수가 <u>잘못</u> 연결된 것을 고르세요.

① one – first

② nine – ninth

③ twelve – twelf

④ thirty – thirtieth

**4** 다음 문장을 우리말로 바르게 옮긴 것을 고르세요.

It's ten to ten.

① 10시이다.

② 9시 10분이다.

③ 10시 10분 전이다.

④ 10시 10분이다.

[5-6] 빈칸에 들어갈 수 <u>없는</u> 것을 고르세요.

**5**

There are _____ carrots on the table.

① ten

② five

③ seventh

④ eleven

**6**

It is the _____ Wednesday of December.

① first

② second

③ three

④ fourth

**7** 빈칸에 들어갈 말이 바르게 짝지어진 것을 고르세요.

- He is the _____ son in his family.
- It is the _____ album by the singer.

① two – six

② two – sixth

③ second – six

④ second – sixth

All our dreams can come true,
if we have the courage to pursue them.

– Walt Disney

**8** 빈칸에 공통으로 들어갈 말을 쓰세요.

A: Is _____ Friday?
B: No, _____ is Thursday.

[9-10] 다음 중 <u>틀린</u> 문장을 고르세요.

**9**
① It is 18 December.
② He is in the third grade.
③ Serena is two years old.
④ Eddie was my first love.

**10**
① It is five fifteen.
② It is close from here.
③ That is a snowy day.
④ It is Thanksgiving Day.

[11-13] 다음 우리말을 영어로 바르게 옮긴 것을 고르세요.

**11**
오늘은 2015년 8월 25일 화요일이다.

① Today is 25 August, Tuesday, 2015.
② Today is 2015, August 25, Tuesday.
③ Today is Tuesday, August 25, 2015.
④ Today is August 25, Tuesday, 2015.

**12**
3시 30분이다.

① It's half to three.
② It's thirty past four.
③ It's three thirteen.
④ It's half past three.

**13**
그녀의 두 번째 손가락은 길다.

① Her two finger is long.
② Her two finger are long.
③ Her second finger is long.
④ Her second finger are long.

**14** 두 문장이 같은 뜻이 되도록 빈칸에 알맞은 말을 쓰세요.

She is ten years old.

→ She is a _____ girl.

**15** 다음 문장에서 <u>틀린</u> 부분을 찾아 바르게 고쳐 쓰세요.

The elevator doesn't stop on the four floor.

_____ → _____

# Word Search

다음 단어의 뜻을 적어보고, 아래에서 찾아보세요.

far _____     gift _____     month _____

weather _____     sunny _____     season _____

```
M  B  X  O  P  Z  P  S  C  Q
Z  G  Z  M  E  F  J  G  Y  I
T  Y  G  I  F  T  U  N  Z  H
S  S  W  Z  L  A  N  F  U  F
S  X  E  Q  W  U  R  N  B  Z
I  Z  A  A  S  T  A  E  Z  U
N  B  T  C  S  E  K  I  P  X
G  T  H  G  M  O  N  T  H  D
Z  R  E  D  Y  N  N  Q  V  T
C  U  R  T  B  O  D  F  F  I
```

초등학생의 영어 친구

# 그래머버디
# GRAMMAR BUDDY

정답 및 해설

# 기초 다지기

**A**  O: rabbit, rose, bed, Seoul
△: we, this, it, I

**B**  1 b  2 a  3 c

**C**  1 명사  2 동사  3 접속사

---

## UNIT 01  be동사의 과거형 1

### CHECK UP  p.10

was, were

### WARM UP  p.11

**A**  3, 6, 7, 8

**B**  1 was  2 were  3 was  4 was
5 were  6 were

### WARM UP  p.13

**A**  O: I, this, that, she, he, it
△: these, you, those, we, they

**B**  1 b  2 b  3 a  4 b

### STEP UP  pp.14~16

**A**  1 is  2 was  3 was  4 was
5 were  6 were  7 was  8 were
1 now(지금)는 현재를 나타내는 표현이므로 be동사의 현
재형이 와야 한다.
4, 5, 7 last … (지난 …), before(전에), yesterday(어제)
는 과거를 나타내는 표현이므로 be동사의 과거형이 와야
한다.

**B**  1 was  2 am  3 is  4 are  5 were
1 주어가 She이고 last night(어젯밤)이라는 과거를 나타
내는 표현이 쓰였으므로 was를 쓴다.
2~4 now(지금), every day(매일), these days(요즘에
는)라는 현재를 나타내는 표현이 쓰였으므로 be동사는
현재형을 쓴다.
5 주어가 They이고 two years ago(2년 전에)라는 과거
를 나타내는 표현이 쓰였으므로 were를 쓴다.

**C**  1 were  2 were  3 was  4 was

---

1~2 주어가 복수명사이므로 were를 쓴다.
4 주어로 셀 수 없는 명사(some water)가 나오므로 was
를 쓴다.

**D**  1 was  2 was  3 were  4 were  5 were
3 주어로 복수명사(lions)가 나오므로 were를 쓴다.

**E**  1 was, short  2 am, tall
3 was, blue  4 is, yellow

**F**  1 was  2 was  3 was
4 were  5 were

### LEAP UP  p.17

**A**  1 You were a good designer.
2 Romeo was in love with Juliet.
3 This was a birthday present from Andy.
4 There were some restaurants on this street.

**B**  1 I was very busy.
2 She was a lovely girl.
3 It was his bicycle.
4 They were at the airport.
5 We were hungry and cold.

---

## UNIT 02  be동사의 과거형 2: 부정문과 의문문

### CHECK UP  p.20

1 ②  2 ②  3 ①

### WARM UP  p.21

**A**  3, 4, 5, 6, 8

**B**  1 ②  2 ②  3 ②  4 ③  5 ②
6 ③  7 ②

### WARM UP  p.23

**A**  2, 4, 6

**B**  1 ①  2 ②  3 ②  4 ①  5 ②  6 ①

### STEP UP  pp.24~26

**A**  1 weren't  2 Was  3 was not
4 wasn't  5 Were  6 weren't
2, 6 last night(지난밤), last class(지난 수업)라는 과거

---

를 나타내는 표현이 쓰였으므로 be동사의 과거형을 쓴다.

**B** 1 was, wasn't    2 was, wasn't
3 were, weren't    4 were, weren't
5 were, weren't
1, 2 was not은 wasn't로 줄여 쓸 수 있다.
3~5 were not은 weren't로 줄여 쓸 수 있다.

**C** 1 wasn't, was    2 weren't, were
3 wasn't, was    4 weren't, were

**D** 1 Was, fast    2 Were, happy
3 was, not, rich    4 were, not, comfortable
1, 2 '…이었니?'라고 과거의 일에 대해 물을 때는 「Was/
Were+주어 …?」의 형태로 쓴다.
3, 4 '…이 아니었다'라는 의미를 나타낼 때는 「주어+was/
were+not …」의 형태로 쓴다.

**E** 1 Was Tony / he was
2 Was Andy / No, he wasn't.
3 Were Jack and Ann / Yes, they were.
1~3 be동사 과거형의 의문문에는 「Yes, 주어+was/
were.」, 「No, 주어+wasn't/weren't.」로 대답할 수 있
다.

**F** 1 sleepy the dog → the dog sleepy
2 wasn't → weren't
3 wasnt → wasn't
4 not was → was not
5 were → was
6 weren't → wasn't

## LEAP UP  p.27

**A** 1 I was not thirsty.
2 Were the tickets expensive?
3 The shoes were not new.
4 Was your mother a lawyer?

**B** 1 The meal was not[wasn't] tasty.
2 Was Jimmy hurt?
3 The children were not[weren't] noisy.
4 Was his grandfather a teacher?

### REVIEW TEST  UNIT 01~02    pp.28~29

1 ④    2 ③    3 wasn't    4 ③    5 ②    6 ④
7 ④    8 ②    9 ④    10 ②    11 wasn't
12 Were the pictures    13 was, not
14 There, were    15 Were → Was

1 ④ 주어가 단수(My mom)이고 last night(어젯밤)이라
는 과거를 나타내는 표현이 쓰인 것으로 보아 be동사는
was가 와야 알맞다.
5 ② 주어가 단수명사(the knife)일 때, be동사 과거형의
의문문에 대한 대답은 「Yes, 주어+was.」 또는 「No, 주
어+wasn't.」로 한다.
8 ②에는 were가, 나머지는 was가 와야 한다.
9 ④ not were를 were not으로 고쳐야 올바른 문장이다.
10 ② yesterday(어제)라는 과거를 나타내는 표현이 쓰였
으므로 Is를 과거형 Was로 고쳐야 올바른 문장이다.
14 '…이 있었다'라는 의미의 「There was/were+주어」
에서, 주어로 복수명사(magazines)가 나오면 were를
쓴다.

### UNIT 03  일반동사의 과거형 1

## WARM UP  p.33

**A** 1 waited    2 hated    3 dropped    4 closed
5 visited    6 studied    7 loved

**B** 1 ①    2 ②    3 ②    4 ①    5 ①
6 ②    7 ①    8 ②

## WARM UP  p.35

**A** 1, 4, 5, 6

**B** 1 ①    2 ②    3 ①    4 ②    5 ①
6 ②    7 ②    8 ①

## STEP UP  pp.36~38

**A** 1 hit    2 put    3 sold    4 tried    5 saw
6 rode    7 had    8 danced    9 helped
10 dropped    11 read    12 listened
13 spoke    14 felt    15 sent    16 made

**B** 1 studied    2 stopped    3 drove
4 arrived    5 swam    6 worked    7 watched
1 「자음+y」로 끝나는 동사는 y를 i로 고치고 -ed를 붙여
과거형을 만든다.
2 「단모음+단자음」으로 끝나는 동사는 맨 뒤 자음을 한 번
더 쓰고 뒤에 -ed를 붙여 과거형을 만든다.
3 drive의 과거형은 drove이다.
4 -e로 끝나는 동사는 뒤에 -d를 붙여 과거형을 만든다.

**C** 1 broke    2 met    3 planned    4 cut
1, 2 break와 meet은 현재형과 과거형이 다른 불규칙 동
사이다.

**4** cut은 현재형과 과거형이 같은 동사이다.

**D**  **1** saw   **2** drank   **3** became   **4** ate   **5** grew
**1~5** 과거형이 -ed로 끝나지 않고 불규칙하게 변하는 동사들이다.

**E**  **1** wake, woke   **2** have, had   **3** do, did

**F**  **1** moved to a new house
**2** painted the walls
**3** bought a big sofa
**4** cleaned the windows

## LEAP UP  p.39

**A**  **1** planted, 그녀는 지난 봄에 나무 한 그루를 심었다.
**2** wore, 그는 어제 파란색 스웨터를 입었다.
**3** used, 그들이 어제 너의 컴퓨터를 사용했다.
**4** went, 그녀는 지난밤에 그 커피숍에 갔다.

**B**  **1** I caught the ball.
**2** She put her bag on the chair.
**3** The baby cried very loudly.
**4** Albert taught English at school in 2012.
**5** My teacher gave homework to us last class.

## UNIT 04  일반동사의 과거형 2: 부정문과 의문문

## CHECK UP  p.42

**1** ①   **2** ②   **3** ①

## WARM UP  p.43

**A**  3, 5, 7, 8

**B**  **1** didn't have   **2** didn't eat   **3** didn't run
**4** didn't like   **5** didn't know   **6** didn't use

## CHECK UP  p.44

**1** Did   **2** Did   **3** Did

## WARM UP  p.45

**A**  1, 2, 3, 5

**B**  **1** didn't   **2** did   **3** didn't
**4** didn't   **5** did

## STEP UP  pp.46~48

**A**  **1** buy   **2** go   **3** didn't   **4** miss
**5** finish   **6** Did
**1, 4** didn't 뒤에는 동사원형이 온다.
**2, 5** 일반동사 과거형의 의문문은 「Did+주어+동사원형 …?」의 형태이다.
**3, 6** last night(지난밤), this morning(오늘 아침)이라는 과거를 나타내는 표현이 쓰였으므로 과거시제가 적절하다.

**B**  **1** didn't, drink
**2** didn't, meet
**3** didn't, write
**4** didn't, wear
**1~4** 일반동사 과거형의 부정문은 「주어+did not+동사원형 ….」의 형태이며, did not은 didn't로 줄여 쓸 수 있다.

**C**  **1** Did, wait   **2** Did, study   **3** Did, start
**4** Did, pay

**D**  **1** didn't, ride, rode   **2** didn't, eat, ate
**3** didn't, stay, stayed

**E**  **1** Did, wear, Yes, she, did
**2** Did, have, No, he, didn't
**3** Did, serve, Yes, he, did
**4** Did, eat, No, they, didn't

**F**  **1** buy   **2** brush   **3** go   **4** answer

## LEAP UP  p.49

**A**  **1** Did he walk the dog?
**2** Ken did not[didn't] enjoy the game.
**3** Did she take off her mask?
**4** I did not[didn't] drink coffee this morning.
**5** The runner did not[didn't] finish the race.

**B**  **1** Did they travel to India?
**2** He didn't do the dishes.
**3** Did she eat my pizza?
**4** I did not[didn't] break the window.

## REVIEW TEST  UNIT 03 ~ 04  pp.50~51

**1** ④   **2** ②   **3** ①   **4** Did   **5** ③   **6** ①
**7** ③   **8** ②   **9** ①   **10** ④   **11** ③   **12** ②
**13** he, did   **14** had   **15** move → moved

**1** ④ drop의 과거형은 dropped이다.

2 ② make의 과거형은 made이다.

3 ① eat의 과거형은 ate이다.

5 ③ 일반동사 과거형의 부정문에서는 did not 뒤에 동사 원형이 온다.

6 ① 문장 끝에 last month(지난달)라는 과거를 나타내는 표현이 쓰였으므로 빈칸에는 과거형 동사가 와야 한다.

10 ④ did를 빼고 lived로 고쳐야 올바른 문장이다.

15 in 2006(2006년에)라는 과거를 나타내는 표현이 쓰였으므로 move를 과거형인 moved로 고쳐야 한다.

## UNIT 05 현재진행형

### WARM UP p.55

**A** 1 b  2 b  3 a  4 b

**B** 1 dying  2 doing  3 cutting  4 writing
5 stopping  6 dancing  7 reading

### WARM UP p.57

**A** 1 ②  2 ③  3 ②  4 ②  5 ①  6 ②  7 ③

**B** 2, 3, 6, 7

### STEP UP pp.58~60

**A** 1 playing  2 need  3 helping
4 talking  5 swimming  6 not speaking
7 Are they
2 need(필요로 하다)와 같이 상태를 나타내는 동사는 진행형으로 쓰지 않는다.
5 「단모음+단자음」으로 끝나는 동사는 맨 뒤 자음을 한 번 더 쓰고 뒤에 -ing를 붙인다.

**B** 1 tying  2 dropping  3 kicking
4 telling  5 raining  6 touching
7 making  8 baking  9 using
10 running  11 flying  12 writing
1 -ie로 끝나는 동사는 ie를 y로 고치고 -ing를 붙인다.
7, 8, 9, 12 -e로 끝나는 동사는 e를 빼고 -ing를 붙인다.

**C** 1 is, he, taking  2 aren't, buying
3 are, climbing  4 is, feeding
2 현재진행형의 부정형은 「be동사+not+동사원형-ing」 형태이다. 이때 be동사와 not을 줄여 쓸 수 있다.
3, 4 현재진행형은 「be동사+동사원형-ing」 형태이다.

**D** 1 is, skating  2 are, watching
3 is, dancing  4 am, holding

**E** 1 Is, smiling, she, is  2 Is, throwing, he, isn't
3 Are, lying, they, are  4 Are, listening, I, am
1~4 현재진행형의 의문문은 「be동사+주어+동사원형-ing …?」의 형태이고, 이에 대한 대답은 「Yes, 주어+be동사.」 또는 「No, 주어+be동사+not.」으로 한다.

**F** 1 is wearing  2 is knocking
3 is waiting  4 is not[isn't] sleeping

### LEAP UP p.61

**A** 1 My mom is cutting the cake.
2 Tiffany is drying her hair.
3 We are not flying a kite.
4 Are they fixing the car?

**B** 1 Leaves are falling.
2 The plane is landing.
3 They are not[They're not / They aren't] playing tennis.
4 Is she going home?

## UNIT 06 형용사

### WARM UP p.65

**A** 1 red, 빨간  2 round, 둥근  3 happy, 행복한
4 sunny, 화창한  5 good, 좋은  6 angry, 화난
7 yellow, 노란  8 small, 작은

**B** 1 big, table  2 beautiful, My mom
3 sweet, peach  4 white, dress
5 cold, The weather  6 new, hairband
7 interesting, The movie

### WARM UP p.67

**A** 1 some  2 any  3 a lot of  4 any
5 Lots of  6 many  7 much

**B** 1 a  2 a, b  3 b  4 b  5 a, b  6 a, b  7 a

### STEP UP pp.68~70

**A** 1 is old  2 lots of  3 much  4 many
5 expensive bag  6 some  7 any
1 형용사(old)는 동사의 뒤에서 주어(My grandfather)를 보충 설명한다.
2 lots of는 '많은'이라는 뜻으로 셀 수 있는 명사와 셀 수 없는 명사 앞에 쓸 수 있다.

**3, 4** many와 much는 둘 다 '많은'이라는 뜻이지만 many는 셀 수 있는 명사 앞에, much는 셀 수 없는 명사 앞에 쓰인다.

**5** 형용사(expensive)가 명사(bag)를 설명할 때는 명사의 앞에 위치한다.

**B** 1 ② 2 ② 3 ③ 4 ③ 5 ③ 6 ② 7 ②

**C** 1 long, short 2 empty, full
3 round, square

**D** 1 some 2 any 3 some 4 any
**1~4** some과 any는 셀 수 있는 명사와 셀 수 없는 명사 앞에 모두 쓰이지만, some은 '약간의', '몇몇의'라는 뜻으로 주로 긍정문에, any는 '약간의 …도', '조금도/전혀(…이 없다)'의 뜻으로 주로 부정문에 쓰인다.

**E** 1 much 2 much 3 many 4 many

**F** 1 blue shirt 2 yellow bicycle
3 some books 4 any birds

## LEAP UP `p.71`

**A** 1 We need a lot of oil.
2 That was a boring game.
3 The girl is kind and pretty.
4 My coat has many buttons.
5 The black bag is expensive.

**B** 1 absent is → is absent
2 new my → my new
3 blanket warm → warm blanket
4 much → many[a lot of/ lots of]
5 many → much[a lot of/ lots of]
6 any → some

### REVIEW TEST UNIT 05 ~ 06 `pp.72~73`

1 ② 2 ④ 3 ③ 4 ② 5 ① 6 ③
7 ④ 8 ④ 9 ③ 10 ② 11 ④
12 ④ 13 swiming → swimming
14 is not[isn't] reading

1 ② 「단모음＋단자음」으로 끝나는 동사는 맨 뒤 자음을 한 번 더 쓰고 뒤에 －ing를 붙이므로 running이 알맞다.
3 ③ 형용사는 소유격(my) 뒤, 명사(bag) 앞에 위치하므로 빈칸에는 my heavy bag이 들어가는 것이 알맞다.
5 ① 빈칸에는 명사(singer)를 꾸미는 형용사가 와야하므로, 동사 like는 들어갈 수 없다.
9 ③ 현재진행형의 부정형은 「be동사＋not＋동사원형－ing」의 형태이다.

## UNIT 07 부사

### WARM UP `p.77`

**A** 1 soon, 곧 2 slowly, 느리게
3 too, 너무 4 well, 잘 5 here, 여기에

**B** 1 sadly 2 carefully 3 loudly
4 easily 5 fast 6 happily 7 simply

### CHECK UP `p.78`

1 always 2 usually 3 often

### WARM UP `p.79`

**A** 1 d 2 c 3 e 4 a 5 b

**B** 1 ② 2 ② 3 ① 4 ① 5 ① 6 ①
7 ② 8 ①

### STEP UP `pp.80~82`

**A** 1 fast 2 safely 3 Sadly 4 warmly
5 is always 6 are never 7 often watch
**5, 6** 빈도부사는 be동사의 뒤에 쓴다.

**B** 1 always 2 usually 3 often
4 sometimes 5 never
**1~5** 빈도부사를 자주 일어나는 순서로 나열하면 always 〉 usually 〉 often 〉 sometimes 〉 never의 순이다.

**C** 1 slowly 2 quietly
3 wonderfully 4 brightly

**D** 1 happily 2 suddenly 3 gently 4 early

**E** 1 usually, sleeps 2 never, eats
3 always, skips 4 is, sometimes, sick
5 is, often, tired
**1~5** 빈도부사는 be동사의 뒤나 일반동사의 앞에 위치한다.

**F** 1 strangely 2 carefully 3 beautifully
4 is usually 5 sometimes cry 6 easily

### LEAP UP `p.83`

**A** 1 high, 그 고양이는 높이 뛰었다.
2 well, 그 소년들은 춤을 잘 췄다.
3 perfectly, 나는 그 곡을 완벽하게 연주한다.
4 Luckily, 운이 좋게도, 그녀는 금메달을 땄다.

Ⓑ 1 He never watches scary movies.
  2 She is always a good friend.
  3 Jim sometimes visits museums.
  4 My parents often help poor people.

## UNIT 08 전치사

### WARM UP p.87

Ⓐ 1 …에(서)   2 … 위에   3 … 안에   4 … 뒤에
  5 … 아래에   6 … 위에,… 너머에   7 … 옆에
  8 … 앞에   9 … 사이에

Ⓑ 1 ③   2 ②   3 ②   4 ②   5 ③

### WARM UP p.89

Ⓐ 1 for   2 to   3 about   4 for
  5 to   6 after   7 with   8 of

Ⓑ 1 in   2 at   3 in   4 at   5 on
  6 at   7 on   8 in   9 on   10 in

### STEP UP pp.90~92

Ⓐ 1 on   2 for   3 at   4 in   5 after
  1 on은 표면 위에 닿아 있는 '…위에'라는 의미이다.
  2 '… 동안'이라는 의미의 전치사는 for이다.
  3 시각을 나타낼 때 쓰는 전치사는 at이다.
  4 in front of는 '… 앞에'라는 의미이다.

Ⓑ 1 on   2 over   3 behind   4 between
  3 '… 뒤에'라는 의미의 전치사는 behind이다.
  4 '… 사이에'라는 의미의 전치사는 between이다.

Ⓒ 1 in, at   2 on, in   3 on, in
  1 월(December) 앞에는 전치사 in이 쓰이고, 시각(9
    p.m.)앞에는 전치사 at이 쓰인다.
  2 특정한 날(Halloween) 앞에는 전치사 on이 쓰이고, 저
    녁(evening) 앞에는 전치사 in이 쓰인다.
  3 날짜 앞에는 전치사 on이 쓰이고, 연도 앞에는 전치사 in
    이 쓰인다.

Ⓓ 1 under the table
  2 before six o'clock
  3 for seven days
  4 at the subway station

Ⓔ 1 in front of   2 in   3 next to   4 behind

Ⓕ 1 in   2 to   3 at   4 with
  1 오전(the morning) 앞에는 전치사 in을 쓴다.

  2 '…으로'라는 의미의 전치사는 to이다.
  4 '…와 함께'라는 의미의 전치사는 with이다.

### LEAP UP p.93

Ⓐ 1 그 공은 담장 너머로 날아갔다.
  2 나는 그 꽃의 이름을 모른다.
  3 우리는 30분 동안 산책했다.
  4 그 식당은 은행과 병원 사이에 있다.

Ⓑ 1 Linda is next to her sister.
  2 Roses are beautiful in May.
  3 I often eat ice cream in summer.
  4 Walter had a party on his birthday.
  5 I go jogging with my sister in the afternoon.

### REVIEW TEST UNIT 07 ~ 08 pp.94~95

1 ②   2 ③   3 ①   4 ④   5 ④   6 ①
7 ③   8 ①   9 ①   10 ②   11 at
12 in front of   13 next to
14 리사는 항상 책을 너무 천천히 읽는다.
15 fastly → fast

1 ② 계절 앞에는 전치사 in을 쓴다.
3 ① 빈칸에는 부사가 와야 한다.
4 ④ 연도(2013) 앞에는 전치사 in을 쓴다.
6 ① 전치사 on은 날짜, 요일, 특정한 날 앞에 쓴다. 시각
   (seven o'clock) 앞에는 at을 쓴다.
8 ① 빈도부사는 be동사의 뒤에 위치한다.
11 전치사 at은 장소 앞에 쓰여 '…에서'의 의미를 나타내거
   나, 특정 시각 앞에 쓰여 '…에'의 의미를 나타낸다.
15 fast는 형용사와 부사의 형태가 같으므로, fastly을
   fast로 고쳐 써야 한다.

## UNIT 09 숫자표현

### WARM UP p.99

Ⓐ 1 b   2 n   3 t   4 t   5 b   6 a   7 e

Ⓑ 1 first   2 three   3 fourth
  4 second   5 first   6 one hundred

### WARM UP p.101

Ⓐ 1 e   2 b   3 d   4 a   5 c   6 f

ⓑ 1 a   2 b   3 a   4 a

## STEP UP pp.102~104

Ⓐ 1 fifteen years old   2 first   3 five   4 ninth
  5 Monday, July 11   6 second
  7 thirty years old   8 seventeen-year-old
  1, 7, 8 나이는 「숫자+years old」 또는 「a/an+숫자-year-old+명사」의 형태로 표현한다.
  2, 4, 6 '··· 번째'와 같이 순서를 나타낼 때 서수를 쓴다.
  5 날짜는 「요일-월-일」의 순서로 쓴다.

Ⓑ 1 nineteen eighty-eight
  2 two thousand sixteen
  3 eighteen forty-five
  4 two thousand six
  5 nineteen ninety-three
  6 two thousand five

Ⓒ 1 first   2 second   3 third   4 fourth

Ⓓ 1 Thursday, November 4, 1970
  2 Saturday, April 5, 2016
  3 Friday, May 15, 2018
  4 Sunday, June 3, 2017
  1~4 영어에서 날짜는 「요일-월-일-연도」의 순서로 쓴다.

Ⓔ 1 April 1   2 twelve   3 two   4 seventieth

Ⓕ 1 eleven years   2 August 27, 2005
  3 twelve-year-old   4 April 8, 2004
  5 thirteen years   6 December 13, 2003

## LEAP UP p.105

Ⓐ 1 우리 안에 원숭이가 세 마리가 있다.
  2 나는 12층에 산다.
  3 올리비아는 6학년이다.
  4 그 열쇠는 첫 번째 서랍에 있다.
  2~4 순서를 나타내는 서수는 '··· 번째'의 의미이다.

Ⓑ 1 Tyler met Kate ten years ago.
  2 My little sister is six years old[a six-year-old girl].
  3 The fifth color of the rainbow is blue.
  4 He entered the school on March 1, 1996.
  5 Thanksgiving Day is on the fourth Thursday of November.

## UNIT 10 비인칭 주어 it

## WARM UP p.109

Ⓐ 1 b   2 d   3 a   4 c   5 e

Ⓑ 1, 4, 5, 6, 7

## WARM UP p.111

Ⓐ 1 b   2 a   3 a   4 b

Ⓑ 1 c   2 d   3 e   4 b   5 a

## STEP UP pp.112~114

Ⓐ 1 It   2 It   3 It   4 It   5 It   6 It
  1~6 날짜와 요일, 거리, 날씨, 계절, 시간 등을 나타낼 때는 비인칭 주어 it을 사용한다.

Ⓑ 1 It, windy   2 It, cloudy
  3 It, sunny   4 It, snowy

Ⓒ 1 to   2 past   3 to   4 past
  1, 3 '··· to ~'는 '~시 ···분 전'의 의미이다.
  2, 4 '··· past ~'는 '~시 ···분'의 의미이다.

Ⓓ 1 It, Thursday   2 It, spring
  3 It, seven, o'clock   4 It, two, kilometers

Ⓔ 1 four, o'clock   2 five   3 nine
  4 twenty, ten   5 ten, three   6 six, forty
  1 정각일 경우 o'clock을 써서 표현하기도 한다.
  3 시간 표현에서 half는 30분을 나타낸다.

Ⓕ 1 It is   2 It is five
  3 It is May.   4 It is Monday.

## LEAP UP p.115

Ⓐ 1 It is Tuesday.
  2 It is winter in Korea.
  3 It is August 28 today.
  4 It is five kilometers from here.

Ⓑ 1 It is Children's Day.
  2 It is eleven o'clock.
  3 It is ten past eight.
  4 It is a rainy day.
  5 It is not far from my house.

## REVIEW TEST UNIT 09 ~ 10 pp.116-117

1 ④　　2 ②　　3 ③　　4 ③　　5 ③　　6 ③

7 ④　　8 it　　9 ①　　10 ③　　11 ③　　12 ④

13 ③　　14 ten-year-old　　15 four → fourth

2 ②의 It은 대명사이고, ①, ③, ④의 It은 비인칭 주어이다.

3 ③ 숫자 12의 서수는 twelfth이다.

4 ③ 시간 표현에서 '… to ~'은 '~시 …분 전'의 의미이다.

5 ③ 빈칸에는 개수를 나타내는 기수를 써야 한다.

6 ③ 빈칸에는 순서를 나타내는 서수를 써야 한다.

9 ① 날짜는 「월-일」 순서로 쓴다.

12 ④ 시간 표현에서 half는 30분의 의미로 쓰이며, '… past ~'은 '~시 …분'의 의미이다.

15 '…번째 층'을 영어로 표현할 때는 서수로 표현한다.

## ★ p. 30 〈나는야 탐험가〉 정답 ★

## 지은이

**NE능률 영어교육연구소**

NE능률 영어교육연구소는 혁신적이며 효율적인 영어 교재를 개발하고
영어 학습의 질을 한 단계 높이고자 노력하는 NE능률의 연구조직입니다.


# 그래머버디 Level 2

| | |
|---|---|
| 펴 낸 이 | 주민홍 |
| 펴 낸 곳 | 서울특별시 마포구 월드컵북로 396(상암동) 누리꿈스퀘어 비즈니스타워 10층 |
| | (주)NE능률 (우편번호 03925) |
| 펴 낸 날 | 2016년 1월 5일 개정판 제1쇄 |
| | 2023년 4월 15일 제15쇄 |
| 전 화 | 02 2014 7114 |
| 팩 스 | 02 3142 0356 |
| 홈 페 이 지 | www.neungyule.com |
| 등 록 번 호 | 제 1-68호 |
| I S B N | 979-11-253-0967-3(63740) |
| 정 가 | 10,000원 |

NE 능률

## 고객센터

교재 내용 문의 : contact.nebooks.co.kr (별도의 가입 절차 없이 작성 가능)
제품 구매, 교환, 불량, 반품 문의 : 02-2014-7114
☎ 전화문의는 본사 업무시간 중에만 가능합니다.

# NE능률 교재 MAP

아래 교재 MAP을 참고하여 본인의 현재 혹은 목표 수준에 따라 교재를 선택하세요.
NE능률 교재들과 함께 영어실력을 쑥쑥~ 올려보세요!
MP3 등 교재 부가 학습 서비스 및 자세한 교재 정보는 www.nebooks.co.kr 에서 확인하세요.

**문법구문**

| 초1-2 | 초3 | 초3-4 | 초4-5 | 초5-6 |
|---|---|---|---|---|
| | 그래머버디 1 | 그래머버디 2 | 그래머버디 3 | Grammar Bean 3 |
| | 초등영어 문법이 된다 Starter 1 | 초등영어 문법이 된다 Starter 2 | Grammar Bean 1 | Grammar Bean 4 |
| | | 초등 Grammar Inside 1 | Grammar Bean 2 | 초등영어 문법이 된다 2 |
| | | 초등 Grammar Inside 2 | 초등영어 문법이 된다 1 | 초등 Grammar Inside 5 |
| | | | 초등 Grammar Inside 3 | 초등 Grammar Inside 6 |
| | | | 초등 Grammar Inside 4 | |

| 초6-예비중 | 중1 | 중1-2 | 중2-3 | 중3 |
|---|---|---|---|---|
| 능률중학영어 예비중 | 능률중학영어 중1 | 능률중학영어 중2 | Grammar Zone 기초편 | 능률중학영어 중3 |
| Grammar Inside Starter | Grammar Zone 입문편 | 1316팬클럽 문법 2 | Grammar Zone 워크북 기초편 | 1316팬클럽 문법 3 |
| 원리를 더한 영문법 STARTER | Grammar Zone 워크북 입문편 | 문제로 마스터하는 중학영문법 2 | 고득점 독해를 위한 중학 구문 마스터 2 | 문제로 마스터하는 중학영문법 3 |
| | 1316팬클럽 문법 1 | Grammar Inside 2 | 원리를 더한 영문법 2 | Grammar Inside 3 |
| | 문제로 마스터하는 중학영문법 1 | 열중 16강 문법 2 | 중학영문법 총정리 모의고사 2 | 열중 16강 문법 3 |
| | Grammar Inside 1 | 고득점 독해를 위한 중학 구문 마스터 1 | 쓰기로 마스터하는 중학서술형 2학년 | 고득점 독해를 위한 중학 구문 마스터 3 |
| | 열중 16강 문법 1 | 원리를 더한 영문법 1 | 천문장 입문 | 중학영문법 총정리 모의고사 3 |
| | 쓰기로 마스터하는 중학서술형 1학년 | 중학영문법 총정리 모의고사 1 | | 쓰기로 마스터하는 중학서술형 3학년 |

| 예비고-고1 | 고1 | 고1-2 | 고2-3 | 고3 |
|---|---|---|---|---|
| 문제로 마스터하는 고등영문법 | Grammar Zone 기본편 1 | 필히 통하는 고등영문법 실력편 | Grammar Zone 종합편 | |
| 올클 수능 어법 start | Grammar Zone 워크북 기본편 1 | TEPS BY STEP G+R Basic | Grammar Zone 워크북 종합편 | |
| 천문장 기본 | Grammar Zone 기본편 2 | 필히 통하는 고등 서술형 실전편 | 올클 수능 어법 완성 | |
| | Grammar Zone 워크북 기본편 2 | | 천문장 완성 | |
| | 필히 통하는 고등영문법 기본 | | | |
| | 필히 통하는 고등 서술형 기본편 | | | |

| 수능 이상/ 토플 80-89 · 텝스 600-699점 | 수능 이상/ 토플 90-99 · 텝스 700-799점 | 수능 이상/ 토플 100 · 텝스 800점 이상 | | |
|---|---|---|---|---|
| TEPS BY STEP G+R 1 | TEPS BY STEP G+R 2 | TEPS BY STEP G+R 3 | | |

초등학생의 영어 친구

# 그래머버디
## WORKBOOK

**2**

# UNIT 01  be동사의 과거형 1

**A** 다음 중 과거를 나타내는 문장에 ✓ 하세요.

1 The street is very busy. ☐

2 The movie was interesting. ☐

3 They are ten years old. ☐

4 My uncle is an excellent chef. ☐

5 There was an old church near here. ☐

6 Alex was in the library an hour ago. ☐

7 They were at the police station last night. ☐

**B** ( ) 안에서 알맞은 것을 고르세요.

1 It (was / were) Sally's raincoat.

2 Allen and I (was / were) good friends.

3 Richard (was / were) very kind to me.

4 I (was / were) late for school yesterday.

5 They (was / were) excited about the trip.

6 Two pairs of socks (was / were) in the box.

7 There (was / were) some bread in the kitchen.

8 There (was / were) many people in the theater.

*Vocabulary*

**A**
street 거리
interesting
재미있는, 흥미로운
excellent 훌륭한
chef 요리사
police station 경찰서

**B**
raincoat 우비
excited 신이 난
trip 여행

C 다음 빈칸에 알맞은 be동사의 과거형을 쓰세요.

1　They _____ very hungry.

2　You _____ a great pianist.

3　The orange juice _____ cold.

4　It _____ my birthday present.

5　That _____ an exciting movie.

6　She _____ very busy last week.

7　My brother _____ sick yesterday.

8　He _____ alone at home last night.

9　Noel and Liam _____ famous singers.

10　There _____ five children at the party.

11　There _____ a good restaurant here before.

12　These jeans _____ too big for him.

13　The weather _____ perfect last weekend.

14　His old apartment _____ near my house.

15　There _____ a lot of new books for teenagers.

**Vocabulary**

C
hungry 배고픈
present 선물
exciting
신나는, 흥미진진한
busy 바쁜
sick 아픈
alone 혼자
restaurant 식당
jeans (청)바지
weather 날씨
perfect 완벽한
weekend 주말
restaurant 식당
apartment 아파트
a lot of 많은
teenager 십대

**D** 빈칸에 알맞은 말을 〈보기〉에서 골라 쓰세요.

〈보기〉   am    are    is    was    were

1  The weather _____ so good yesterday.

2  This soup _____ warm an hour ago.

3  The boy _____ a baby seven years ago.

4  The wind _____ very strong yesterday.

5  My cousins _____ in New Zealand now.

6  The twins _____ at home two hours ago.

7  There _____ a bench in the backyard before.

8  There _____ some water in the bottle ten minutes ago.

9  There _____ red roses in the garden last year.

10  The game _____ very popular these days.

Vocabulary

D
ago … 전에
strong 강한
cousin 사촌
twins 쌍둥이
bench 벤치
backyard 뒤뜰
before 전에
bottle 병
last year 작년
game 게임, 경기
popular 인기 있는
these days 요즘에는

다음 우리말과 같은 뜻이 되도록 빈칸에 알맞은 말을 쓰세요.

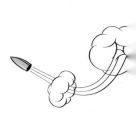

1 그것은 나의 실수였다.

→ It _____ my mistake.

2 그 도시는 매우 조용했다.

→ The city _____ very quiet.

3 저것은 내가 가장 좋아하는 인형이다.

→ That _____ my favorite doll.

4 그들은 어제 너무 피곤했다.

→ They _____ too tired yesterday.

5 어젯밤에는 달이 밝았다.

→ The moon _____ bright last night.

6 학생들은 예의 바르고 영리했다.

→ The students _____ polite and smart.

7 이 사과는 신선하고 맛있다.

→ These apples _____ fresh and delicious.

8 예전에 은행 근처에 서점이 있었다.

→ There _____ a bookstore near the bank
before.

## Vocabulary

mistake 실수
city 도시
quiet 조용한
bright 밝은
polite 예의 바른
fresh 신선한
delicious 맛있는
bookstore 서점
bank 은행

# UNIT 02  be동사의 과거형 2: 부정문과 의문문

**A** 다음 문장에서 not이 들어갈 위치에 ✓ 하세요.

*Vocabulary*

Ⓐ

textbook 교과서
surprised 놀란
dentist 치과 의사
sunny 화창한
neighbor 이웃

1  It ① was ② your ③ textbook.

2  The parents ① were ② surprised.

3  Her ① name ② was ③ Emma.

4  Mr. Black ① was ② a dentist.

5  The weather ① was ② nice ③ and sunny.

6  Kate and ① Larry ② were ③ my neighbors.

**B** 다음 문장을 의문문으로 바꿀 때 빈칸에 알맞은 말을 쓰세요.

Ⓑ
bug 벌레
angry 화난
wise 지혜로운, 현명한
novel 소설
boring
재미없는, 지루한

1  There was a bug.    →  _____ _____ a bug?

2  They were angry.    →  _____ _____ angry?

3  She was wise.    →  _____ _____ wise?

4  The novel was very boring.

  →_____ _____ _____ very boring?

5  Those were his toys.

  →_____ _____ his toys?

6  This camera was new.

  →_____ _____ _____ new?

**C** ( ) 안에서 알맞은 것을 고르세요.

1   (Was / Were) the grape juice sweet?

2   A: Were you happy?    B: Yes, I (am / was).

3   The questions (was / were) not easy.

4   The boxes (was / were) not big and heavy.

5   (It were / Was it) cold and windy yesterday?

6   I (wasn't / weren't) late for school yesterday.

7   (Was / Were) Bill and David on the school bus?

8   His smartphone (was not / not was) in the car.

9   A: Was the street clean?    B: No, (it's not / it wasn't).

10  My grandfather (wasn't / weren't) in the hospital.

11  A: Were the nurses kind?    B: Yes, they (was / were).

12  A: Was the sandwich delicious?    B: No, it (was / wasn't).

13  (Were / Was) there a cat on the sofa?

14  She (weren't / wasn't) at the party last night.

*Vocabulary*

**C**
grape juice
포도 주스
sweet 달콤한
question 질문, 문제
easy 쉬운
heavy 무거운
windy
바람이 많이 부는
smartphone
스마트폰
be in the hospital
입원 중인

**D** 다음 문장을 (  ) 안의 지시대로 바꿔 쓰세요.

## Vocabulary

**D**
idea 생각
kid 아이
noisy 시끄러운
subway 지하철
crowded 붐비는
victory 승리
actor 배우
stage 무대
tourist 관광객
castle 성
bed 침대

1   It was my idea. (부정문)

→ _____

2   The kids were noisy. (의문문)

→ _____

3   The subway was very crowded. (부정문)

→ _____

4   They were happy with the victory. (부정문)

→ _____

5   There were five actors on the stage. (의문문)

→ _____

6   The room was big and clean. (부정문)

→ _____

7   There were a lot of tourists in the castle. (의문문)

→ _____

8   There was an alarm clock next to the bed. (의문문)

→ _____

E 다음 우리말과 같은 뜻이 되도록 ( ) 안의 말을 바르게 배열하세요.

## Vocabulary

E
expensive 비싼
hat 모자
comfortable 편안한
food 음식
letter 편지
library 도서관
grandparents
조부모님

1   그 모자는 비쌌니? (was / expensive / the hat)

→ _____

2   그 의자는 편안했니? (the chair / comfortable / was)

→ _____

3   음식이 전혀 없었다. (any food / not / there / was)

→ _____

4   그것은 그녀의 편지가 아니었다. (her / not / it / letter / was)

→ _____

5   그 책들은 새 것이 아니었다. (new / were / the books / not)

→ _____

6   저것은 그들의 집이 아니었다.

(that / house / was / their / not)

→ _____

7   그들은 도서관에 없었다.

(they / the library / not / in / were)

→ _____

8   네 조부모님이 편찮으셨니?

(sick / grandparents / your / were)

→ _____

# UNIT 03 일반동사의 과거형 1

**A** 다음 문장의 시제로 알맞은 것에 ✓ 하세요.

1  I saw Jane in a restaurant.　□ 현재 □ 과거

2  We often listen to the radio.　□ 현재 □ 과거

3  She has a new computer.　□ 현재 □ 과거

4  They looked very surprised.　□ 현재 □ 과거

5  The woman made cupcakes.　□ 현재 □ 과거

6  Julie and James are at a party.　□ 현재 □ 과거

7  Dad came home late last night.　□ 현재 □ 과거

*Vocabulary*

A
often 자주
listen to …을 듣다
surprised 놀란

**B** 다음 동사의 과거형으로 알맞은 것을 고르세요.

1  put  (put / puted)

2  begin (began / beganed)

3  give  (gived / gave)

4  buy  (buyed / bought)

5  visit  (visit / visited)

6  arrive (arrived / arriveed)

7  stop  (stoped / stopped)

B
put 놓다, 두다
begin 시작하다
give 주다
buy 사다
visit 방문하다
arrive 도착하다
stop 멈추다

**C** 〈보기〉와 같은 관계가 되도록 빈칸에 알맞은 말을 쓰세요.

*Vocabulary*

C
feel 느끼다
see 보다
teach 가르치다
plan 계획하다
tell 말하다
move
움직이다, 옮기다
cut 자르다
stand 서다

〈보기〉  go – went

1  do    – _____       8  tell  – _____

2  feel  – _____       9  move – _____

3  get   – _____      10  eat   – _____

4  see   – _____      11  study – _____

5  teach – _____      12  sit   – _____

6  read  – _____      13  cut   – _____

7  plan  – _____      14  stand – _____

**D** 주어진 동사를 과거형으로 써서 문장을 완성하세요.

C
know 알다
answer 해답, 답
drop 떨어뜨리다
shop 가게
open (문을) 열다
pasta 파스타
together 함께, 같이

1  know   She _____ the answer.

2  drop   Mandy _____ the dish.

3  work   The farmer _____ hard.

4  open   The shop _____ last week.

5  have   Joey _____ pasta for lunch.

6  play   We _____ baseball together.

**E** 우리말과 같은 뜻이 되도록 〈보기〉의 단어를 이용하여 문장을 완성하세요.

*Vocabulary*

**E**

call 전화하다

find 찾다, 발견하다

sleep 자다

laugh 웃다

break 깨다

loudly 큰 소리로

taxi driver 택시 기사

carefully 조심스럽게

under … 아래에

department store 백화점

〈보기〉 call    meet    find    write

　　　 sleep    laugh    break    drive

1　그 소년은 창문을 깨뜨렸다.

　→ The boy _____ the window.

2　학생들은 크게 웃었다.

　→ The students _____ loudly.

3　나는 제니에게 이메일을 썼다.

　→ I _____ an e-mail to Jenny.

4　그 택시 기사는 조심스럽게 운전했다.

　→ The taxi driver _____ carefully.

5　나는 어제 톰에게 전화를 걸었다.

　→ I _____ Tom yesterday.

6　나는 침대 밑에서 열쇠를 찾았다.

　→ I _____ the key under the bed.

7　우리는 백화점에서 만났다.

　→ We _____ in the department store.

8　그는 어젯밤 잠을 푹 잤다.

　→ He _____ well last night.

주어진 단어를 빈칸에 알맞은 형태로 쓰세요.

1  have  Henry usually _____ lunch with his friends.
         But he _____ lunch alone yesterday.

2  live  My family _____ in Seoul last year.
         But we _____ in Busan now.

3  go    Megan usually _____ to bed at 9 p.m.
         But she _____ to bed at 11 p.m. last night.

4  learn  Ronan _____ French two years ago.
          He _____ Japanese this year.

5  begin  The meeting usually _____ at 2 p.m.
          But it _____ at 4 p.m. last week.

6  want  Mike _____ a bike for his birthday before.
         Now he _____ a computer.

7  wake  My mother usually _____ up at 6 a.m.
         But she _____ up at 9 a.m. last Sunday.

8  watch  Ben _____ an action movie yesterday.
          But he usually _____ comedy movies.

usually 보통, 대개
alone 혼자
go to bed
자다, 자러 가다
learn 배우다
French 프랑스어
Japanese 일본어
meeting 회의
want 원하다
wake up 잠에서 깨다
action movie
액션 영화
comedy movie
코미디 영화

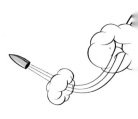

# UNIT 04  일반동사 과거형 2: 부정문과 의문문

**A** 다음 빈칸에 알맞은 말을 〈보기〉에서 골라 쓰세요.

〈보기〉  don't    doesn't    didn't

1  I _____ know Sandra before.

2  We _____ have an umbrella now.

3  She _____ ride a roller coaster yesterday.

4  They _____ go camping last weekend.

5  He _____ take violin lessons these days.

**B** 다음 문장을 의문문으로 바꿀 때 빈칸에 알맞은 말을 쓰세요.

1  Nate drank coffee.
→ _____ Nate _____ coffee?

2  Cathy bought a bag.
→ _____ Cathy _____ a bag?

3  He missed the bus.
→ _____ he _____ the bus?

4  You broke the plate.
→ _____ you _____ the plate?

5  My friends lied.
→ _____ my friends _____?

*Vocabulary*

**A**
ride 타다
roller coaster
롤러코스터
weekend 주말
take a lesson
수업을 받다
these days
요즘에는

**B**
miss 놓치다
plate 접시
lie 거짓말하다

C　다음 질문에 알맞은 대답을 바르게 연결하세요.

1　Did she call you?　•　•a　Yes, she did.

2　Did he play the game?　•　•b　No, I didn't.

3　Did you read the book?　•　•c　No, it didn't.

4　Did they eat breakfast?　•　•d　Yes, we did.

5　Did we find the answer?　•　•e　Yes, they did.

6　Did the dog bark loudly?　•　•f　No, he didn't.

*Vocabulary*

C
answer 해답, 대답
bark 짖다
loudly 큰 소리로

D　(　) 안에서 알맞은 것을 고르세요.

1　Did she (sleep / slept) late?

2　(Was / Did) he move to London?

3　They didn't (do / did) their homework.

4　Lucy didn't (enjoy / enjoys) the movie.

5　(Were / Did) they clean the living room?

6　(Do / Did) you pass the test yesterday?

7　She (doesn't / didn't) live in Korea in 2013.

8　The boy (wasn't / didn't) brush his teeth last night.

D
move
옮기다, 이사하다
do one's homework
숙제를 하다
enjoy 즐기다
pass
통과하다, 합격하다
test 시험
brush one's teeth
양치질하다

주어진 문장을 부정문과 의문문으로 바꿀 때 빈칸에 알맞은 말을 쓰세요.

1 The train arrived on time.

(부정문) → _____ on time.

(의문문) → _____ on time?

2 Emma took a walk in the forest.

(부정문) → _____ a walk in the forest.

(의문문) → _____ a walk in the forest?

3 We knew her phone number.

(부정문) → _____ her phone number.

(의문문) → _____ her phone number.

4 Lisa told the secret to him.

(부정문) → _____ the secret to him.

(의문문) → _____ the secret to him?

5 Ethan invited me to the party.

(부정문) → _____ me to the party.

(의문문) → _____ me to the party?

6 They thought about the question.

(부정문) → _____ about the question.

(의문문) → _____ about the question?

## Vocabulary

E

train 기차

on time
시간을 어기지 않고,
정각에

take a walk 산책하다

forest 숲

phone number
전화번호

secret 비밀

invite 초대하다

think 생각하다

question 질문, 문제

다음 우리말과 같은 뜻이 되도록 ( ) 안의 말을 바르게 배열하세요.

**Vocabulary**

borrow 빌리다
swim 수영하다
pool 수영장
fruit 과일
reporter 기자
child 아이, 어린이
become …이 되다
feed 먹이를 주다
wash 씻다

1 그들은 영어 공부를 했니? (they / study / English / did)

→ _____

2 그가 내 선물을 좋아했니? (my / did / like / present / he)

→ _____

3 나는 그녀의 펜을 빌리지 않았다.

(pen / borrow / I / not / did / her)

→ _____

4 너는 수영장에서 수영을 했니?

(you / swim / did / in the pool)

→ _____

5 우리는 과일을 사지 않았다. (buy / fruit / didn't / we)

→ _____

6 그 아이는 기자가 되지 않았다.

(a reporter / the child / become / didn't)

→ _____

7 잭이 그 고양이에게 먹이를 주었니?

(feed / Jack / did / the cat)

→ _____

8 로라는 설거지를 하지 않았다.

(did / the dishes / Laura / wash / not)

→ _____

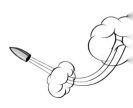

# UNIT 05  현재진행형

## A 우리말과 일치하는 문장을 고르세요.

**Vocabulary**

A
exercise 운동하다

1  그는 운전 중이다.
   - a   He drives a car.
   - b   He is driving a car.

2  벤은 매일 운동을 한다.
   - a   Ben exercises every day.
   - b   Ben is exercising every day.

3  그 아기는 잘 웃는다.
   - a   The baby smiles a lot.
   - b   The baby is smiling a lot.

4  나는 음악을 듣고 있다.
   - a   I listen to music.
   - b   I'm listening to music.

## B ( ) 안에서 알맞은 것을 고르세요.

B
fly 날다
high 높이
help 돕다
take a test
시험을 보다
arrive 도착하다
station 역

1  The birds (are / do) flying high.

2  He is (help / helping) an old lady.

3  Is (Jane eating / eating Jane) her cake?

4  I'm (wait / waiting) for your answer.

5  The student (take / is taking) a test now.

6  We (not are / are not ) having a party.

7  The train (is / does) arriving at the station.

## C 다음 문장에서 not이 들어갈 위치에 ✓ 하세요.

1  She ① is ② playing ③ the guitar.

2  I'm ① making ② coffee ③ for you.

3  The men ① are ② painting ③ the wall.

4  My brother is ① taking ② a shower ③.

5  They are ① eating ② lunch ③ together.

6  Mr. White ① is ② carrying ③ a suitcase.

*Vocabulary*

C
make 만들다
paint 페인트칠하다
wall 벽
take a shower
샤워를 하다
carry 들고 있다
suitcase 여행 가방

## D 다음 동사를 「동사원형 –ing」 형태로 바꿔 쓰세요.

1  go _____

2  fix _____

3  stop _____

4  die _____

5  set _____

6  try _____

7  put _____

8  say _____

9  invite _____

10  climb _____

11  begin _____

12  leave _____

13  drop _____

14  dance _____

D
fix 고치다
die 죽다
set 놓다
try 노력하다
put 놓다, 두다
climb 오르다
leave 떠나다

다음 주어진 말을 이용하여 빈칸에 알맞은 말을 쓰세요.

Vocabulary

E
newspaper 신문
bench 벤치
cry 울다
laugh 웃다
kid 아이
draw 그리다
cook 요리하다
run 달리다
do the laundry
빨래를 하다
floor 바닥, 층
lie 거짓말하다
truth 사실

1  read (X)    Mom __isn't reading__ a newspaper.
   watch (O)   She __is watching__ the news on TV.

2  sit (X)     Chloe _____ on a bench.
   stand (O)   She _____ .

3  cry (X)     The kids _____ .
   laugh (O)   They _____ loudly.

4  study (X)   The students _____ math.
   draw (O)    They _____ pictures.

5  bake (X)    Ms. Simpson _____ bread.
   cook (O)    She _____ rice for dinner.

6  run (X)     Mason and I _____ .
   walk (O)    We _____ .

7  do (X)      Adam _____ the laundry.
   clean (O)   He _____ the floor.

8  lie (X)     The man _____ .
   tell(O)     He _____ the truth.

다음 우리말과 같은 뜻이 되도록 (  ) 안의 말을 바르게 배열하세요.

*Vocabulary*

catch 잡다
brush 빗질하다
school uniform
교복
stage 무대
use 사용하다
sofa 소파

1   그들은 택시를 잡고 있니? (are / a taxi / they / catching)

→ _____

2   앤은 머리를 빗는 중이다. (Ann / her hair / brushing / is)

→ _____

3   나는 주스를 마시고 있지 않다.

(I / juice / not / drinking / am)

→ _____

4   그는 교복을 입고 있다.

(a school uniform / is / he / wearing)

→ _____

5   그녀는 무대에서 노래하고 있니?

(she / on the stage / is / singing)

→ _____

6   그들은 컴퓨터를 쓰고 있지 않다.

(they / the computer / not / are / using)

→ _____

7   아빠는 소파에 누워 있다. (is / on / Dad / the sofa / lying)

→ _____

8   루크는 음악을 듣는 중이다.

(to / Luke / listening / is / music)

→ _____

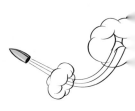

# UNIT 06 형용사

**A** 다음 문장에서 형용사에 O 하고, 그 뜻을 쓰세요.

1  It was a windy day.                    _____

2  She is a kind woman.                   _____

3  That's an expensive coat.              _____

4  The kid is so smart.                   _____

5  They were very thirsty.                _____

6  I don't have yellow boots.             _____

7  My brother is tall.                    _____

*Vocabulary*

A
woman 여자, 여성
coat 코트, 외투
boots 부츠

**B** 우리말과 일치하는 영어 표현을 고르세요.

1  신선한 우유        (fresh milk / milk fresh)

2  빨간 사과          (a red apple / red an apple)

3  그의 작은 개        (small his dog / his small dog)

4  그 어린 소년        (the boy little / the little boy)

5  나의 새 신발        (new my shoes / my new shoes)

6  큰 정원            (a large garden / large a garden)

B
fresh 신선한
little 어린
large 큰
garden 뜰, 정원

## C 다음 빈칸에 들어갈 수 <u>없는</u> 것을 고르세요.

1 _____ juice   ① an   ② some   ③ much

2 the _____ train   ① fast   ② next   ③ drive

3 a _____ story   ① funny   ② her   ③ exciting

4 _____ children   ① some   ② much   ③ lots of

5 a _____ sweater   ① warm   ② mine   ③ long

6 my _____ friend   ① play   ② new   ③ best

7 a _____ street   ① quiet   ② go   ③ clean

*Vocabulary*

C
funny
웃기는, 재미있는
exciting
신나는, 흥미진진한
story 이야기
children 아이들
warm 따뜻한
sweater 스웨터
quiet 조용한
street 거리

## D 두 문장이 같은 뜻이 되도록 빈칸에 many나 much 중 알맞은 것을 쓰세요.

1 Do you have a lot of comic books?

→ Do you have _____ comic books?

2 We have a lot of snow in winter.

→ We have _____ snow in winter.

3 There were a lot of tomatoes in the basket.

→ There were _____ tomatoes in the basket.

4 The woman has lots of money in her purse.

→ The woman has _____ money in her purse.

D
comic book 만화책
snow 눈
winter 겨울
tomato 토마토
basket 바구니
purse 지갑

**E** ( ) 안에서 알맞은 것을 고르세요.

1 I don't have (any / some) questions.

2 I drink (many / much) water every day.

3 There are (much / a lot of) trees in this park.

4 She bought (some / any) meat at the market.

5 We have (many / much) homework today.

6 There isn't (some / any) cheese in the refrigerator.

7 The bus was very crowded with (some / many) people.

**F** 두 문장이 같은 뜻이 되도록 빈칸에 알맞은 말을 쓰세요.

1 This is a famous model.

→This model _____ _____.

2 It was a comfortable chair.

→The chair _____ _____.

3 That was an easy game.

→That game _____ _____.

4 She is a polite woman.

→The woman _____ _____.

 다음 우리말과 같은 뜻이 되도록 〈보기〉에서 알맞은 말을 골라 쓰세요.

Vocabulary

G
village 마을
diamond
다이아몬드
story 이야기
weather 날씨

〈보기〉 dirty   tiny   weak   sour
       hard   cloudy   round   boring

1   그 마을은 아주 작다.

→ The village _____.

2   다이아몬드는 단단하다.

→ Diamonds _____.

3   이 오렌지는 시다.

→ This orange _____.

4   저 소년은 몸이 약하다.

→ That boy _____.

5   그의 장갑은 더러웠다.

→ His gloves _____.

6   그 식탁은 둥글다.

→ The table _____.

7   그 이야기는 지루했다.

→ The story _____.

8   오늘은 날씨가 흐리다.

→ The weather _____ today.

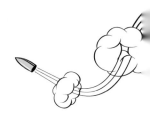

# UNIT 07 부사

**A** 다음 중 부사를 고르세요.

1. ① leave ② picnic ③ now

2. ① kindly ② sunny ③ peaceful

3. ① brave ② island ③ honestly

4. ① usual ② quick ③ often

5. ① ugly ② loudly ③ enjoy

6. ① here ② great ③ tiny

7. ① round ② soon ③ happiness

*Vocabulary*

A
peaceful 평화로운
brave 용감한
usual 평상시의
quick 빠른
happiness 행복

**B** 다음 문장에서 부사에 O 하고, 그 뜻을 쓰세요.

1. This skirt is too short. _____

2. Dinner is almost ready. _____

3. These candies are so sweet. _____

4. The students spoke quietly. _____

5. Thomas drove his car fast. _____

6. The old man walked slowly. _____

7. Sadly, our team lost the game. _____

B
ready 준비가 된
speak
이야기하다, 말하다
drive 운전하다
old 늙은, 나이 많은
walk 걷다
team 팀
lose 지다, 패하다

**C** 〈보기〉와 같은 관계가 되도록 빈칸에 알맞은 말을 쓰세요.

〈보기〉  easy – easily

1  deep   – _____

2  early   – _____

3  quick   – _____

4  clear   – _____

5  happy  – _____

6  high    – _____

7  heavy  – _____

8  slow    – _____

9  fast     – _____

10  sudden – _____

11  good    – _____

12  careful  – _____

*Vocabulary*

C
deep 깊은
early 이른
quick 빠른
clear 분명한
high 높은
heavy 무거운
slow 느린
sudden 갑작스러운
careful 조심스러운

**D** 다음 빈도부사가 들어갈 위치에 ✓ 하세요.

1   never       I ① tell ② lies.

2   sometimes   The girl ① is ② rude.

3   always      The sun ① rises ② in the east.

4   usually     He ① plays ② soccer after school.

5   often       We ① go ② to Chinese restaurants.

6   always      She ① is ② kind to everybody.

D
rude 무례한
rise 오르다; *뜨다
east 동쪽
everybody 모두

**E** ( ) 안에서 알맞은 것을 고르세요.

1 Cheetahs run (fast / fastly).

2 Jeremy is a (polite / politely) student.

3 The baby (is often / often is) ill.

4 He bought a (real / really) expensive watch.

5 The park (is sometimes / sometimes is) crowded.

6 The balloons flew (high / highly) in the sky.

7 John (is never / isn't never) late for work.

8 I (have always / always have) breakfast.

9 We (go usually / usually go) camping on weekends.

10 The airplane landed (safe / safely) at the airport.

11 (Lucky / Luckily), I got two tickets for the concert.

12 Bella (always / never) helps me. She is very kind.

13 Jake (often / never) eats peanuts. He hates them a
   lot.

*Vocabulary*

**E**
cheetah 치타
ill 아픈
watch 시계
balloon 풍선
go camping
캠핑을 가다
weekend 주말
concert 콘서트
help 돕다
land 착륙하다
airport 공항
peanut 땅콩
a lot 정말

*Vocabulary*

**F**
perfect 완벽한
hard 열심히 하는
life 삶

1  Greg spoke perfect Japanese.

→ Greg spoke Japanese _____.

2  My father is a hard worker.

→ My father works _____.

3  Julian is a good dancer.

→ Julian dances _____.

4  Peter and Ariana lived a happy life.

→ Peter and Ariana lived _____.

**G** 다음 우리말과 같은 뜻이 되도록 빈칸에 알맞은 빈도부사를 쓰세요.

**G**
road 도로, 길
forget 잊다
password 암호

1  그들은 보통 아홉 시에 잠자리에 든다.

→ They _____ go to bed at nine.

2  이 도로는 월요일에 항상 붐빈다.

→ This road is _____ crowded on Mondays.

3  나는 그 암호를 자주 잊어버린다.

→ I _____ forget the password.

4  우리 아빠는 가끔 우리에게 저녁을 해주신다.

→ My father _____ cooks dinner for us.

# UNIT 08 전치사

## A 다음 빈칸에 들어갈 말로 알맞은 것에 ✓ 하세요.

1 We watched a movie about _____.

☐ well          ☐ behind          ☐ the universe

2 This is a picture of _____.

☐ go            ☐ red             ☐ him

3 They had lunch with _____.

☐ Patrick       ☐ together        ☐ delicious

4 The bank is in front of _____.

☐ their         ☐ close           ☐ the hospital

5 There is a family photo on _____.

☐ take          ☐ big             ☐ the wall

*Vocabulary*

A
universe 우주
picture 사진, 그림
together 함께
photo 사진
wall 벽

## B 다음 표현과 우리말을 바르게 연결하세요.

1 on the table          •          • a    탁자 앞에

2 under the table       •          • b    탁자 뒤에

3 next to the table     •          • c    탁자 옆에

4 behind the table      •          • d    탁자 위에

5 in front of the table •          • e    탁자 아래에

C 다음 빈칸에 알맞은 말을 〈보기〉에서 골라 쓰세요.

〈보기〉  in  at  on

1 _____ June

2 _____ 2020

3 _____ winter

4 _____ May 1

5 _____ the afternoon

6 _____ night

7 _____ Tuesday

8 _____ 9:30 p.m.

9 _____ two o'clock

10 _____ New Year's Day

D ( ) 안에서 알맞은 것을 고르세요.

1 He sent an e-mail (to / in) James.

2 We are sitting (on / of) the bench.

3 I took a shower (about / before) dinner.

4 Jeremy is standing (behind / over) the tree.

5 She drew a picture (with / at) her father.

6 There are many tourists (at / over) the airport.

7 The baby took a nap (for / with) three hours.

**E** 다음 빈칸에 공통으로 들어갈 전치사를 쓰세요.

1 We have a test _____ Monday.

 I was born _____ November 20.

2 I usually listen to music _____ the evenings.

 He had a bottle of water _____ his bag.

3 My father watches the news _____ night.

 Alex stayed _____ home last weekend.

4 I gave some flowers _____ my teacher.

 Ms. White drove her car _____ the mall.

5 I went shopping _____ my mother.

 The boy played _____ his dog in the garden.

**F** 다음 빈칸에 알맞은 전치사를 쓰세요.

1 I visited Paris _____ June 22.

2 I went to the Eiffel Tower _____ the morning.
 It was wonderful!

3 And I took a boat trip _____ the Seine River.

4 I enjoyed the trip _____ an hour.

5 There were many beautiful bridges _____ the river.

*Vocabulary*

**E**
test 시험
born 태어나다
bottle 병
stay 머무르다
give 주다
mall 쇼핑몰

**F**
visit 방문하다
Paris 파리
wonderful
아주 멋진
boat 배, 보트
trip 여행
enjoy 즐기다
bridge 다리

우리말과 같은 뜻이 되도록 빈칸에 알맞은 전치사를 쓰세요.

*Vocabulary*

lamp 램프, 전등
arrive 도착하다
roll 구르다, 굴러가다
lake 호수
talk
말하다, 이야기하다

1 소파 옆에 전등이 있다.

→ There is a lamp _____ the sofa.

2 스쿨버스가 여덟 시 전에 도착했다.

→ The school bus arrived _____ eight o'clock.

3 공은 그의 발 사이로 굴러갔다.

→ The ball rolled _____ his feet.

4 선물 상자가 침대 아래에 있었다.

→ A gift box was _____ the bed.

5 새들이 호수 위로 날고 있다.

→ The birds are flying _____ the lake.

6 학생들은 그들의 미래에 대해 이야기했다.

→ The students talked _____ their futures.

7 그는 방과 후에 수영 강습을 받는다.

→ He takes swimming lessons _____ school.

8 집 앞에 있는 흰 차가 보이니?

→ Do you see the white car _____ the house?

# UNIT 09 숫자표현

**A** 〈보기〉와 같은 관계가 되도록 빈칸에 알맞은 말을 쓰세요.

〈보기〉　4 – four – fourth

1　2　–　_____　–　_____

2　3　–　_____　–　_____

3　5　–　_____　–　_____

4　8　–　_____　–　_____

5　9　–　_____　–　_____

6　11　–　_____　–　_____

7　12　–　_____　–　_____

8　20　–　_____　–　_____

9　26　–　_____　–　_____

10　30　–　_____　–　_____

11　31　–　_____　–　_____

12　44　–　_____　–　_____

13　67　–　_____　–　_____

14　100　–　_____　–　_____

15　400　–　_____　–　_____

**B** 알맞은 연도를 찾아 연결하세요.

*Vocabulary*

1  1492  •                    • a  sixteen hundred

2  1600  •                    • b  two thousand two

3  1984  •                    • c  fourteen ninety-two

4  1877  •                    • d  nineteen eighty-four

5  2002  •                    • e  two thousand eighteen

6  2018  •                    • f  eighteen seventy-seven

**C** 우리말과 일치하는 것에 O 하세요.

1  3월 22일        (March 22 / 22 March)

2  11월 11일        (November 11 / December 11)

3  8월 3일 월요일    (Monday 3, August / Monday, August 3)

4  5월 15일 토요일   (Saturday, May 15 / 15 May, Saturday)

5  1949년 7월 16일  (1949, July 16 / July 16, 1949)

6  2008년 6월 21일  (2008, June 21 / June 21, 2008)

**C**
March 3월
July 7월
Monday 월요일
August 8월
Saturday 토요일

**D** 다음 우리말과 일치하는 영어 표현에 ✓ 하세요.

*Vocabulary*

**D**
grade 학년
visit 방문
daughter 딸
magazine 잡지

1  3학년
   ☐ third grade          ☐ three grade

2  나의 첫 방문
   ☐ my one visit         ☐ my first visit

3  5층
   ☐ the fifth floor      ☐ the five floor

4  7월 4일 일요일
   ☐ Sunday 4, July       ☐ Sunday, July 4

5  첫째 딸
   ☐ the one daughter     ☐ the first daughter

6  둘째 주 금요일
   ☐ the two Friday       ☐ the second Friday

7  잡지 여덟 권
   ☐ eight magazines      ☐ the eighth magazine

8  두 살 아기
   ☐ a two-year-old baby  ☐ a two years old baby

**E** 주어진 숫자를 빈칸에 알맞은 형태로 쓰세요.

1  Tina is _____ years old. (13)

2  I live on the _____ floor. (17)

3  Mr. and Mrs. Martin have _____ kids. (3)

4  Ted is the _____ son in his family. (2)

5  Nick has _____ sisters and a brother. (2)

6  Rita read _____ books last month. (5)

7  Jennifer is a _____ grade student. (4)

8  There are _____ cups of tea on the table. (8)

9  The Earth is the _____ planet from the Sun. (3)

10  Today is my mother's _____ birthday. (46)

11  The doctor's office is on the _____ floor. (10)

12  It's the _____ day at my new school. I feel nervous. (1)

13  A baseball team has _____ players on the field. (9)

*Vocabulary*

**E**
Earth 지구
planet 행성
nervous 불안해하는
player 선수
field 경기장

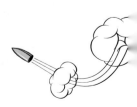

# UNIT 10  비인칭 주어 it

**A** 밑줄 친 it의 쓰임으로 알맞은 것에 ✓ 하세요.

1  It is very windy.　　　☐ 대명사　☐ 비인칭 주어

2  What time is it?　　　☐ 대명사　☐ 비인칭 주어

3  It is a birthday gift.　☐ 대명사　☐ 비인칭 주어

4  It's Thanksgiving Day.　☐ 대명사　☐ 비인칭 주어

5  It's forty-five dollars.　☐ 대명사　☐ 비인칭 주어

6  Is it far from your office?　☐ 대명사　☐ 비인칭 주어

7  It was a beautiful scene.　☐ 대명사　☐ 비인칭 주어

## Vocabulary

**A**

windy
바람이 많이 부는
Thanksgiving Day
추수감사절
scene 풍경

**B** 밑줄 친 It이 나타내는 것을 〈보기〉에서 찾아 그 기호를 쓰세요.

〈보기〉　ⓐ 날짜　ⓑ 요일　ⓒ 시간　ⓓ 계절　ⓔ 날씨　ⓕ 거리

1  It's spring now.　　　_____

2  It was a snowy day.　　_____

3  It's November 30.　　 _____

4  It is seven kilometers.　_____

5  It's twenty to three.　 _____

6  It wasn't Wednesday.　_____

**B**
spring 봄
snowy
눈이 많이 내리는
kilometer 킬로미터
Wednesday 수요일

**C** 다음 질문에 알맞은 대답을 〈보기〉에서 찾아 그 기호를 쓰세요.

*Vocabulary*

**C**
fall 가을
close 가까운
date 날짜
season 계절

〈보기〉    ⓐ It's fall.

ⓑ It's Thursday.

ⓒ It's September 15.

ⓓ It was close from here.

1  How far was it?            _____

2  What's the date?           _____

3  What season is it?         _____

4  What day is it today?      _____

**D** 다음 중 알맞은 시간 표현을 찾아 바르게 연결하세요.

**D**
half 반, 절반

1  08:50 •                    • a  It is five twenty.

2  12:30 •                    • b  It is ten to nine.

3  02:15 •                    • c  It is seven thirty.

4  06:55 •                    • d  It is eleven o'clock.

5  03:25 •                    • e  It is five to seven.

6  11:00 •                    • f  It is half past twelve.

7  05:20 •                    • g  It is three twenty five.

8  07:30 •                    • h  It is two fifteen.

**E** 다음 문장과 같은 뜻이 되도록 빈칸에 알맞은 말을 쓰세요.

*Vocabulary*

1  It's eight o'clock. → It's _____.

2  It's ten past five. → It's _____ _____.

3  It's half past nine. → It's _____ _____.

4  It's ten to twelve. → It's _____ _____.

5  It's nine fifty-five. → It's _____ to ten.

6  It's six forty. → It's _____ to seven.

7  It's three twenty.
   → It's twenty _____ _____.


**F** 다음 우리말과 같은 뜻이 되도록 빈칸에 알맞은 말을 쓰세요.

1  오늘은 금요일이다.
   → _____ _____ Friday today.

2  2시 정각이다.
   → _____ _____ two o'clock.

3  날씨가 흐리다.
   → _____ _____ cloudy.

4  여기서 멀다.
   → _____ _____ far from here.

**F**
Friday 금요일
cloudy
구름이 잔뜩 낀

Ⓖ 다음 우리말과 같은 뜻이 되도록 ( ) 안의 말을 바르게 배열하세요.

**Vocabulary**

Ⓖ
hot 더운, 뜨거운
cold 추운
outside 밖에
rainy 비가 많이 오는
Saturday 토요일
meter
미터(길이의 단위)

1  세 시 정각이다. (o'clock / is / three / it)

   → _____

2  오늘은 덥다. (is / today / hot / it)

   → _____

3  밖은 추웠다. (outside / it / cold / was)

   → _____

4  비가 오는 날이다. (is / a / day / it / rainy)

   → _____

5  토요일이 아니었다. (not / Saturday / was / it)

   → _____

6  6시 20분 전이다. (six / is / twenty / it / to)

   → _____

7  7시 30분이다. (is / half / seven / it / past)

   → _____

8  여기서 50m 거리이다. (from / it / is / fifty meters / here)

   → _____

# ★ 정답 ★

## UNIT 01 be동사의 과거형 1    PP.2-5

**A** 2, 5, 6, 7

**B** 1 was   2 were   3 was   4 was
   5 were   6 were   7 was   8 were

**C** 1 were   2 were   3 was   4 was
   5 was   6 was   7 was   8 was
   9 were   10 were   11 was
   12 were   13 was   14 was   15 were

**D** 1 was   2 was   3 was   4 was
   5 are   6 were   7 was
   8 was   9 were   10 is

**E** 1 was   2 was   3 is   4 were
   5 was   6 were   7 are   8 was

## UNIT 02 be동사의 과거형 2: 부정문과 의문문    PP.6-9

**A** 1 ②   2 ②   3 ③   4 ②   5 ②   6 ③

**B** 1 Was, there   2 Were, they
   3 Was, she   4 Was, the, novel
   5 Were, those   6 Was, this, camera

**C** 1 Was   2 was   3 were   4 were
   5 Was it   6 wasn't   7 Were
   8 was not   9 it wasn't   10 wasn't
   11 were   12 wasn't   13 Was
   14 wasn't

**D** 1 It was not[wasn't] my idea.
   2 Were the kids noisy?
   3 The subway was not[wasn't] very
     crowded.
   4 They were not[weren't] happy with
     the victory.
   5 Were there five actors on the stage?

6 The room was not[wasn't] big and
  clean.
7 Were there a lot of tourists in the
  castle?
8 Was there an alarm clock next to the
  bed?

**E** 1 Was the hat expensive?
   2 Was the chair comfortable?
   3 There was not any food.
   4 It was not her letter.
   5 The books were not new.
   6 That was not their house.
   7 They were not in the library.
   8 Were your grandparents sick?

## UNIT 03 일반동사의 과거형 1    PP.10-13

**A** 1 과거   2 현재   3 현재   4 과거
   5 과거   6 현재   7 과거

**B** 1 put   2 began   3 gave   4 bought
   5 visited   6 arrived   7 stopped

**C** 1 did   2 felt   3 got   4 saw   5 taught
   6 read   7 planned   8 told
   9 moved   10 ate   11 studied
   12 sat   13 cut   14 stood

**D** 1 knew   2 dropped   3 worked
   4 opened   5 had   6 played
   7 opened

**E** 1 broke   2 laughed   3 wrote
   4 drove   5 called   6 found   7 met
   8 slept

**F** 1 has, had   2 lived, live
   3 goes, went
   4 learned[learnt], learns
   5 begins, began   6 wanted, wants
   7 wakes, woke   8 watched, watches

## UNIT 04 일반동사의 과거형 2: 부정문과 의문문 pp.14-17

**A** 1 didn't  2 don't  3 didn't  4 didn't
5 doesn't

**B** 1 Did, drink  2 Did, buy
3 Did, miss  4 Did, break
5 Did, lie

**C** 1 a  2 f  3 b  4 e  5 d  6 c

**D** 1 sleep  2 Did  3 do  4 enjoy
5 Did  6 Did  7 didn't  8 didn't

**E** 1 The train did not[didn't] arrive,
Did the train arrive
2 Emma did not[didn't] take,
Did Emma take
3 We did not[didn't] know,
Did we know
4 Lisa did not[didn't] tell, Did Lisa tell
5 Ethan did not[didn't] invite,
Did Ethan invite
6 They did not[didn't] think,
Did they think

**F** 1 Did they study English?
2 Did he like my present?
3 I did not borrow her pen.
4 Did you swim in the pool?
5 We didn't buy fruit.
6 The child didn't become a reporter.
7 Did Jack feed the cat?
8 Laura did not wash the dishes.

## UNIT 05 현재진행형 pp.18-21

**A** 1 b  2 a  3 a  4 b

**B** 1 are  2 helping  3 Jane eating
4 waiting  5 is taking  6 are not  7 is

**C** 1 ②  2 ①  3 ②  4 ①  5 ①  6 ②

**D** 1 going  2 fixing  3 stopping
4 dying  5 setting  6 trying
7 putting  8 saying  9 inviting
10 climbing  11 beginning
12 leaving  13 dropping  14 dancing

**E** 1 isn't reading, is watching
2 isn't sitting, is stading
3 aren't crying, are laughing
4 aren't studying, are drawing
5 isn't baking, is cooking
6 aren't running, are walking
7 isn't doing, is cleaning
8 isn't lying, is telling

**F** 1 Are they catching a taxi?
2 Ann is brushing her hair.
3 I am not drinking juice.
4 He is wearing a school uniform.
5 Is she singing on the stage?
6 They are not using the computer.
7 Dad is lying on the sofa.
8 Luke is listening to music.

## UNIT 06 형용사 pp.22-25

**A** 1 windy, 바람 부는  2 kind, 친절한
3 expensive, 값이 비싼  4 smart, 똑똑한
5 thirsty, 목이 마른  6 yellow, 노란
7 tall, 키가 큰

**B** 1 fresh milk  2 a red apple
3 his small dog  4 the little boy
5 my new shoes  6 a large garden

**C** 1 ①  2 ③  3 ②  4 ②
5 ②  6 ①  7 ②

**D** 1 many  2 much  3 many  4 much

**E** 1 any  2 much  3 a lot of  4 some

5 much   6 any   7 many

F 1 is, famous   2 was, comfortable
  3 was, easy   4 is, polite

G 1 is tiny   2 are hard   3 is sour
  4 is weak   5 were dirty   6 is round
  7 was boring   8 is cloudy

## UNIT 07 부사               PP.26-29

A 1 ③   2 ①   3 ③   4 ③   5 ②
  6 ①   7 ②

B 1 too, 너무   2 almost, 거의
  3 so, 너무나, 정말로   4 quietly, 조용하게
  5 fast, 빠르게   6 slowly, 천천히
  7 Sadly, 슬프게도

C 1 deeply   2 early   3 quickly
  4 clearly   5 happily   6 high
  7 heavily   8 slowly   9 fast
  10 suddenly   11 well   12 carefully

D 1 ①   2 ②   3 ①   4 ①   5 ①   6 ②

E 1 fast   2 polite   3 is often
  4 really   5 is sometimes   6 high
  7 is never   8 always have
  9 usually go   10 safely   11 Luckily
  12 always   13 never

F 1 perfectly   2 hard   3 well   4 happily

G 1 usually   2 always
  3 often   4 sometimes

## UNIT 08 전치사               PP.30-32

A 1 the universe   2 him   3 Patrick
  4 the hospital   5 the wall

B 1 d   2 e   3 c   4 b   5 a

C 1 in   2 in   3 in   4 on   5 in
  6 at   7 on   8 at   9 at   10 on

D 1 to   2 on   3 before   4 behind
  5 with   6 at   7 for

E 1 on   2 in   3 at   4 to   5 with

F 1 on   2 in   3 to   4 for   5 over

G 1 next to   2 before   3 between
  4 under   5 over   6 about   7 after
  8 in front of

## UNIT 09 숫자표현               PP.34-37

A 1 two, second
  2 three, third
  3 five, fifth
  4 eight, eighth
  5 nine, ninth
  6 eleven, eleventh
  7 twelve, twelfth
  8 twenty, twentieth
  9 twenty-six, twenty-sixth
  10 thirty, thirtieth
  11 thirty-one, thirty-first
  12 forty-four, forty-fourth
  13 sixty-seven, sixty-seventh
  14 one hundred, one hundredth
  15 four hundred, four hundredth

B 1 c   2 a   3 d   4 f   5 b   6 e

C 1 March 22
  2 November 11
  3 Monday, August 3
  4 Saturday, May 15
  5 July 16, 1949
  6 June 21, 2008

Ⓓ 1 third grade
   2 my first visit
   3 the fifth floor
   4 Sunday, July 4
   5 the first daughter
   6 the second Friday
   7 eight magazines
   8 a two-year-old baby

Ⓔ 1 thirteen   2 seventeenth
   3 three   4 second   5 two   6 five
   7 fourth   8 eight   9 third
   10 forty-sixth   11 tenth
   12 first   13 nine

## UNIT 10 비인칭 주어 it    pp.38-41

Ⓐ 1 비인칭 주어   2 비인칭 주어   3 대명사
   4 비인칭 주어   5 대명사   6 비인칭 주어
   7 대명사

Ⓑ 1 ⓓ   2 ⓔ   3 ⓐ   4 ⓕ   5 ⓒ   6 ⓑ

Ⓒ 1 ⓓ   2 ⓒ   3 ⓐ   4 ⓑ

Ⓓ 1 b   2 f   3 h   4 e   5 g   6 d
   7 a   8 c

Ⓔ 1 eight   2 five, ten   3 nine, thirty
   4 eleven, fifty   5 five   6 twenty
   7 past, three

Ⓕ 1 It, is   2 It, is   3 It, is   4 It, is

Ⓖ 1 It is three o'clock.
   2 It is hot today.
   3 It was cold outside.
   4 It is a rainy day.
   5 It was not Saturday.
   6 It is twenty to six.
   7 It is half past seven.
   8 It is fifty meters from here.